Tell Me, Grandmother

Tell Me, Grandmother

*Traditions, Stories, and Cultures
of Arapaho People*

VIRGINIA SUTTER

University Press of Colorado

Published by the University Press of Colorado
5589 Arapahoe Avenue, Suite 206C
Boulder, Colorado 80303

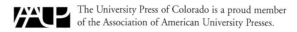 The University Press of Colorado is a proud member
of the Association of American University Presses.

The University Press of Colorado is a cooperative publishing enterprise supported, in part,
by Adams State College, Colorado State University, Fort Lewis College, Mesa State College,
Metropolitan State College of Denver, University of Colorado, University of Northern Colorado,
and Western State College of Colorado.

The paper used in this publication meets the minimum requirements of the American National
Standard for Information Sciences—Permanence of Paper for Printed Library Materials.
ANSI Z39.48-1992

Library of Congress Cataloging-in-Publication Data

Sutter, Virginia J.
Tell me, grandmother : traditions, stories, and cultures of Arapaho people / Virginia J. Sutter.
p. cm.
Includes bibliographical references.
ISBN 0-87081-784-1 (hardcover : alk. paper) — ISBN 0-87081-785-X (pbk. : alk. paper)
1. Goes In Lodge, ca. 1830–1876. 2. Arapaho women—Biography. 3. Arapaho Indians—History.
4. Arapaho Indians—Social life and customs. I. Title.
E99.A7G647 2004
978.004'97354'0092—dc22

2004010394

Design by Daniel Pratt
Typesetting by Laura Furney

To my three children, Jim, Dennis, and Vicki;
my eight grandchildren, Jaimie, Jon, Jeff, Keli,
Michael, Ryan, Matthew, and Ben;
and my three great-grandchildren,
Jacob, Joshua, and Madison.

Contents

Acknowledgments

My thanks to Harold Smith, Elder, one of the Four Spiritual Old Men, and Sun Dance Priest of the Northern Arapaho Tribe, and also my special friend;

To Margaret Coel, noted author, who understands and appreciates the value of Arapaho storytelling;

To my grandson, Indian way, Gordon Yellowman, Southern Cheyenne Chief, and Sun Dance Priest of the Southern Cheyenne, who supported me in providing both oral and written histories of our families in the traditional manner of our Cheyenne brothers;

To my family who have patiently waited for this glimpse into the history of their genesis;

To two wonderful traditional people who were helpful in the creation of this book but who have passed on to the other world:

First, Anthony Sitting Eagle, an Elder and one of the Four Spiritual Old Men of the Northern Arapaho Tribe. Anthony loved a good story and throughout his lifetime was the central character in many of them. The people he loved will long remember his wonderful sense of Indian humor and his dedication to the traditional Arapaho way.

Second, Laura Revere, an Elder and devoted mother and grandmother who became the essence of extended family to many young people. Laura had the honor of sitting in the Sun Dance Lodge and held the traditional ways close to her heart. It was my pleasure to sit next to her in the sweat lodge, and in the sacred dark of the lodge among the rising prayer mists, we feel her presence still.

Tell Me, Grandmother

Prologue

When my father, Arlo Amos, requested that I return to the reservation in 1969, we had many discussions about our tribe, the Northern Arapaho, and the various members of our family. I became so intrigued with the history of my great-grandmother, Goes In Lodge, wife of Chief Sharp Nose, that I began to gather information about her life. The most valued information came from the Elders, and many stories came from older members of our family. I gathered still other material from books, wills, military records, newspapers, and probate proceedings.

As I searched the past, Grandmother Goes In Lodge became very real to me, and I longed to sit down with her in the Wind River Mountains and listen to her stories, to have the soft whisper of the breeze through the pine boughs mingle with our conversation as she took me back through time to tell me of her life. I also longed to share moments of my life with her. I have written this book as a series of imagined conversations to help my family learn more of those relatives who struggled with survival during the 1800s. It is also written for people who have an interest in learning more about the true culture and traditions of Arapaho Indians.

Arapaho Indians, as do many other Plains tribes, have special storytellers. Storytellers know how to capture the interest of their audience and teach a lesson at the same time. There are the warrior's endless repetitions of moments of valor on the battlefield, shared with others that they might sleep peacefully at night. There are the creation myths and legends of our beginning. Such tales may take as long as seven days and seven nights to relate.

And there are the grandmother stories. We need to listen carefully to these stories because they are much like Mother Nature's nuts and fruits. The outside shell of words may be unattractive and perhaps even displeasing as it reveals the harsh factual events, but the inner part of the story—easily missed if not given rapt attention—is what holds the lessons of life, revealing the miracles of life given to us freely by the Creator. These stories may start at any point in history and end when they are finished. They may resume at a later date to continue with additional characters and events.

That is how this book is written, intertwining the lives of a great-grandmother and her great-granddaughter, as if two people were telling each other their stories, leaving the mystery of who will continue this story as history unfolds in the next century.

I cannot sit with my great-grandmother and share our stories, but through my research I believe our conversations have a strong basis in truth. I like to think her spirit has watched over the writing of this book and that she approves of my efforts. My wish is that as people read these stories, they will have a better understanding of our Arapaho culture and traditions.

Chapter One

Tell me, Grandmother Goes In Lodge, what were your first memories of life on this earth? Could it have been the sounds of an Arapaho camp, the low murmur of conversation among your family as they gathered for an evening meal? Or was it some traumatic event that brought you rudely into the reality of life with resounding effects that stayed in your memory for a lifetime? Perhaps it was the pounding of hooves heralding the return of warriors from battle or voices raised in alarm, shouting a warning to move camp in the face of an enemy attack. I would like to know more, Grandmother, of your beginning.

Granddaughter, our people did not write of my time; our history was oral. The history of the Arapaho is traditionally important, and a true telling of events must be done. During my lifetime we were unable to write things down, so the storytellers had to remember everything. This was no small task. Many events took place within each generation. The stories that explained the sacred rituals (such as morning prayers) in daily life had to be passed on to the young people. There were tales of creation and of the early days before the Arapaho lived in the Plains country. There were stories of war parties and battles. The storyteller described skirmishes that might highlight an individual's outstanding bravery in protecting the tribe, as well as major battles in which many warriors lost their lives.

Family histories became an important part of storytelling as generations mixed and mingled among the bands. It was necessary to know family structures, as marrying one's relatives was strictly forbidden. The stories also followed the tribe's traveling patterns, reminding people of the cycles of dry years with little rain and noting the years when grazing and game were plentiful. The weather stories assisted scouts in providing safe winter and summer campsites for the tribe. Each time a story was told it helped the storyteller's memory as he continued to repeat the events. In your time, Granddaughter, many of our stories have been forgotten, but some have been saved by individual family elders.

Yes, Granddaughter, the *Hinon'eino* used the spoken word to tell of our myths, rituals, and history. We depend upon our storytellers. In my time, because of their role as preservers of the past, the storytellers merited an honored place in our villages. It takes a good memory, imagination, and speaking ability to be a storyteller. Arapaho mythology is rich in detail and imagery. Our people believe in the legends of the Sacred Pipe, the story of the arrival of fire among the Plains Indians, and the struggle of the Arapaho against the mischievous and invisible "Little People." We do not speak lightly of the Little People or discuss them at length because to do so could bring them around for an unexpected visit.

The stories told by our generation evoke supernatural powers. They call on the spirits of *Nooku,* the Rabbit; *Koo'oh,* the Trickster Coyote; *Hooxei,* the Wolf; *Nih'oo3oo,* the Spider; *Be'enoo,* the Turtle; and others. These animals often play the role of helper, meddler, or teacher. Through these stories our children learn about the relationship between animals and human beings. Lives of our people have been saved during severe weather and lack of food by the generosity of our four-legged friends. Lesson stories are told with a trace of humor, which Indian people enjoy.

A good example of this, Granddaughter, is seen in the Coyote, or Trickster, stories. The Trickster stories are told for fun and to help children accept a funny person's behavior. The Trickster is a famous figure in Indian storytelling. He has unusual powers; in fact, he assumes he has the same power as the Creator. In a way he is an animal, but in another way he is human. He is thought to be clever, but he always gets into trouble because he thinks he is smarter than everybody else.

Our people like a good joke, even at our own expense. Elders enjoy exchanging stories about their relatives, and humor softens the truth of our failures in meeting life's challenges.

In my time, Granddaughter, our storytellers were treated with great respect, and they took their lifetime pledge seriously. When someone needed a story, that person approached the storytellers ceremoniously. They were fed a special meal consisting of four main items: coffee, dried meat, chokecherry gravy, and fry bread. Before the storytelling started, all participants took part in a cleansing cedar ceremony. This was done by sprinkling medicine on a hot cottonwood charcoal, and the people then blessed themselves with the smoke.

Our Cheyenne brothers had a similar practice of approaching the storyteller for a tale, which I will share with you as it was told to me. This ritual was followed especially for holy stories. The storyteller would smooth the ground in front of him with his hand and make two marks in it with his right thumb, two with his left, and a double mark with both thumbs together. Then he would rub his hands, pass his right hand up his right leg to his waist, and touch his left hand and pass it up his right arm to his breast. He did the same thing with the other hand, going up the other side. Then he touched the marks on the ground with both hands, rubbed his hands together, and passed them over his head and all over his body. That meant the Creator had made human beings' bodies and limbs as he made the earth, and the Creator was witness to what was to be told.

The heart of Arapaho stories, legends, and myths reflects the view that we as people are created equal to all things, alive or without life, and we share the earth as partners under the watchful eye of the Creator.

Grandmother, our last recognized storyteller of Arapaho history, Mike Brown of the Arapaho community on the Wind River Reservation, passed away in 1979 at age eighty-two. Mike Brown was recognized, by tribal members and others, as having a special talent for Indian humor, which delighted all ages. Humor was an important part of his storytelling, but he knew the serious side of history as well. Mike especially enjoyed being called upon to teach the children in the schools with his storytelling. Even the teachers and office personnel would gather around with rapt attention as he spoke. Mike's rendition of historic battles was related with truth and colorful descriptions. His story of Weasel Bear of the *Ba'sawunena,* a division of the Northern Arapaho, becoming keeper of the Sacred Pipe in 1892 was told with respect and hushed reverence for the event's traditional significance. Mike remained an active storyteller and was available to the people until his death.

I had the honor, Grandmother, of knowing Mike and his second wife, Frances, in the 1960s when I first returned to the reservation. Frances made me a beautiful set of moccasins and leggings beaded in traditional Arapaho colors of red, black, blue, and yellow and told me to wear them with pride at the gatherings of our people. This I have done for the past thirty years. When I wear them, Grandmother, I think of the history we lost with Mike Brown's passing. Each passing of an elder leaves us in sorrow, not only for the individual but also for the pieces of our history that are forever lost.

When I was young I heard the Old Ones tell how the Arapaho lived east of the Mississippi, and over time we migrated to the northwestern corner of Minnesota and possibly into the eastern provinces of Canada. As we entered the West we remained close to our brothers, the Cheyenne, who share our identity of habitation. The Great Plains became our territory, as far west as the Rocky Mountains and east beyond the Missouri.

Granddaughter, when I was born many changes were taking place in the outside world east of the Rockies. I was too young to understand, Grand-

daughter, the terrible years our tribe would experience as events took place in our country. Many events would affect my lifetime.

I was born around 1830, less than thirty years after the Lewis and Clark Expedition, when white man's history would be written across the territories—before the end of our prairie freedom. Lewis and Clark met many Indian tribes as they journeyed across our lands in the period 1803–1806. They gave our leaders peace medals. But they did not enter into treaty negotiations with our chiefs. Our people lived a free and easy life on the prairie. Our lives seemed quiet and unhurried at this time. There was never a great rush to do something. Basically, we ate when we were hungry, slept when we were tired and needed to rest. The sun told us when to begin and end our days. All family members had their tasks and knew their roles and obligations. The women were nurturers and caretakers; the men were hunters and protectors, and they had ceremonial responsibilities. The Arapaho were a social group and enjoyed gatherings where goods were exchanged. The men looked forward to trading horses and buffalo robes for the white man's goods brought by Cheyenne traders. Lewis and Clark were the first to call our people the Blue Bead Indians.

Grandmother, I know the descendants of Sacajawea, the Shoshone woman who led Lewis and Clark across the territory. One of Sacajawea's great-granddaughters became my friend in the early 1990s. Although we live far apart, she is still my friend.

I read about a significant action in the white world that affected our future as a recognized Indian nation. In 1818 the House Committee on Appropriations reported: "In the present state of our country one of two things seems necessary. Either that those sons of the forest should be moralized or exterminated. Put into the hands of their children the primer and the hoe, and they will naturally, in time, take hold of the plow."

Granddaughter, how little these white men knew of the Hinon'eino. When I was young, our warriors fought our enemies, but they did so in honest battle, then left to go their separate ways. It was not our way to ask others to change their culture. We are all children of Mother Earth, each free to seek our own path. As the four-leggeds, the fish, and the fowl are free to seek their own way.

Grandmother, still another significant event that severely affected our people took place in 1824. The organized efforts of missionary societies and churches and the conscience of the federal government brought about the establishment of the Bureau of Indian Affairs within the United States War Department. This event fostered a destructive dependence on the white people and their ways.

Granddaughter, I was born in the middle of what were later called the "Treaty Years," 1788 to 1871. Our people often camped in the territory at the edge of the Rocky Mountains. The white people were coming in large numbers. In the beginning we were curious about these people and their strange ways, but as time passed we became frightened by their aggressive attitude. Ours is a giving and sharing nature. For white men there was never enough. They continued to reach for more of everything. We were unable to continue our way of life and let them live theirs, as we had done with other tribes that came after our hunting lands. Even the ways of war, as we knew them, changed. Soon we were fighting not only for our lives but also for our way of life.

How difficult it would have been for you, Grandmother, to understand that elsewhere in the land, white people were already planning reservations where Indian people would be forced to live without consideration of tribal models of justice. It was still too early for our tribes to realize how traumatic the years were to become as the effort was made to separate us from our culture and traditional ways.

As the white man moved further into our country, fighting became expensive for the government, and treaty making ensued. When treaties were made with our people in the 1850s, the white people were greatly concerned about "civilizing" Indians who were unprepared for the changes affecting their way of life. Many Indians spoke only a few words of English and depended on translators for accurate interpretations. They barely understood what the treaty process was all about.

A treaty suggests an equal bargaining position between parties, Grandmother, but our people were at a disadvantage during these negotiations. The treaties were written in English, the interpreters were usually biased, and the truth was rarely evident.

One of the most dramatic treaty signings in which our people took part was the Treaty of Fort Laramie in 1851. Besides the Arapaho, delegations of Sioux, Cheyenne, Crow, Assiniboin, Gros Ventres, Mandan, and Arikara were called to the council. Over 10,000 Indians camped along the Platte at Horse Creek, thirty-six miles downriver from Fort Laramie. The council proceedings were a slow process, allowing time for translating the treaty into the various tribal languages. How well any of the Indians understood the treaty in its entirety is difficult to know. Indian languages are descriptive, and brief statements of fact were not likely to be clearly conveyed through translation.

Grandmother, one major legal battle during the treaty era was the 1831 case *Cherokee Tribe v. the State of Georgia*. This case dealt with federal guardianship over Indian affairs and the states' encroachment on Indian lands in violation of the tribes' treaty rights. This case would also affect our people in the recognition of future treaty rights. In this case Chief Justice John Marshall characterized Indian nations as "domestic dependent nations," creating a new law where none had previously existed. The case clearly stated the notions of Indian tribes' internal sovereignty and their immunity from state intrusion. This internal sovereignty, as established by a treaty, operated as a shield that defeated attempts by state officials to exercise authority over Indians and their lands and property. As time passed, the "domestic dependent" Indian nations became exempt from state taxation, political regulation, administrative intrusion, and preemption, as well as from criminal and civil state laws. Today, *Cherokee Tribe* is still the most important court decision in federal Indian law.

Granddaughter, I was born in the years of great beaver destruction. White men searched Indian lands for *hébesi,* beaver, one of the four-leggeds we respect for its beautiful fur and contribution to our medicines. The white men did not see the contribution this animal made to Mother Earth in its care and love for the rivers and small creeks leading to larger bodies of water. They missed the beauty of beaver dam construction and the natural control of overgrowth. They saw only the pelts used in making hats coveted by the rich.

Even so, I was happy and secure in the early years of my life. They were my learning years. My playmates and I learned the value of natural things and their importance to our life on the prairie. We were secure within our extended families. Our cousins were our brothers and sisters, and we were taught to respect our elders and regard them as our grandparents. We rejoiced in the feeling of freedom as we were accepted into the lodges of our relatives and friends throughout the camp.

Grandmother, the Old Ones tell me children were most likely born in a tepee on the prairie. Or if the tribe was traveling, babies may have been delivered in the fresh air of the windswept sagebrush plains. The female members of the family and perhaps relatives of the husband's family attended the mother. What excitement must have run through the camp when Grandfather Winds carried the baby's first cries throughout the village or traveling band. A new baby was always heralded as a gift of the Creator and a blessing to all.

You were given a wonderful name, Grandmother Goes In Lodge, and I wonder how your naming came about. There are many wonderful ways to receive a name among the *Hinon'eino.* Often, names originate in the unusual, something associated with a brave or charitable deed. Or a baby might be named after an activity affiliated with war. The name could come from a mysterious event or object or from a strange animal in a vision. Some children were named so they would have a long and happy life.

Granddaughter, my mother told me I was born outside the main family lodge in a smaller lodge prepared especially for my birth. When I arrived, my grandmother took me outside and held me high in the air for all to see. She then carried me with great ceremony into my new lodge to be dressed and presented to my family and my new world. That is why I became known as "Goes In Lodge." In later years I was also called "Woman Going In." It is not unusual for our people to change their name or to be known by more than one name.

Our birthing process reflected our responsibility to the Creator for the miracle of birth and followed a traditional path with respect to natural events. From the time a mother became with child, we had many practices and taboos to protect the baby from harm until it entered the world.

One taboo was against having twins. For that reason the expectant mother never ate the portion of meat called "twins," which are tenderloin strips of meat next to the backbone of the buffalo. We believed in this taboo for many reasons. First, during the approach of a warring tribe, mothers could manage only one infant at a time as the camp prepared to flee. Second, mothers understood that their babies should be spaced six years apart. During hunting season, when camps moved frequently, a mother could have one youngster clinging to her as she carried an infant, but more would prevent her from doing her share of the labor. She had to help move camp, tend to freshly killed meat, and gather food and water. I accept that our people had reasons for this belief.

Another taboo was that we never drank hot water or coffee during pregnancy to guard against a difficult birth.

In my search to better understand your life, Grandmother, the Old Ones, both male and female, have shared many things with me. And I am grateful, Grandmother, but I wish I could have had the opportunity to sit with you on Mother Earth, somewhere serene in a mountain meadow that would be much the same as it was during your time, and listen to your stories. And I could share mine with you.

I would tell you of the discrimination and prejudice that hovered over me like a dark cloud during the early years of my life. Perhaps you could help me understand why this happened to those of us who were forced to share another's culture, one we did not understand and one that did not care to understand our ways. Why should our traditions or the color of our skin cause such dishonor and disrespect?

To talk of these things with you, I would choose a special place of natural beauty. Someplace unspoiled by the intrusion of ugly poles stripped of their dignity as trees, hung with wire, and stretched shamelessly across the prairie—heralding the growth and progress of another culture. For our visit I would choose the sandy beach of Moccasin Lake high in the Wind River Mountains. This lake has been a favorite fishing and camping spot for our family for many years. It lies in a sheltered glen surrounded by rock cliffs and a beautiful pine forest. As you walk along the edge of the lake, you can look down and see the fish swimming through the crystal-clear water. If you sit quietly in the sun, you will find the solitude and beauty of the lake bring serenity to your soul. This is where we could enjoy a wonderful visit.

Here in the Wind River country the mountains and valleys are unchanging, as opposed to the rivers, marching to their own inner drum, changing course in the spring when their banks—bulging with spring run-off—give them the strength to show their independence. Sadly, Grandmother, our beautiful wilderness is often crisscrossed by dusty roads and black strips of unyielding surface where our little four-leggeds die under the wheels of careless drivers rushing everywhere and nowhere.

Since our visit is not to be on this earth or in this time, I will take this time to tell you of my life, and I rely on the Old Ones to help me learn of your life. They tell me that after you were born, your umbilical cord was put away to dry. Your mother preserved it in a beaded amulet stuffed with sweetgrass. These small beaded bags were usually shaped to represent the long-lived lizard or turtle to help you reach maturity. My grandchildren have their amulets. They are of buckskin and beaded in Arapaho colors.

Granddaughter, when I was a baby my beaded amulet was attached to my cradle board, and later it was fastened to my clothing. It was with great pride that families made sure each child received a cradle board at birth.

Arapaho cradle. Courtesy, National Anthropological Archives, Smithsonian Institution (neg. no. 81-3319-14).

I was unaware of the days I spent in this wonderful, safe, and secure nest. The cradle board was beautifully decorated with quillwork by my mother's friends under the direction of the Seven Old Women specially chosen for their knowledge. As they worked, they prayed for me to have a long and happy life. The younger women waited outside the lodge but joined in the prayers. How wonderful it was to be received into such a happy family and to be loved by all. I would snuggle down in my wrappings, bouncing along on my mother's back as she gathered wood and prepared the family meal over an outdoor fire. Many times my cradle hung from the branch of a tree while my mother gathered berries, keeping one eye on the trail to watch for bears that might have staked out the berry patch as their own. This is where I first learned that trees talk, their soft leaves whispering to one another. They gently sang me lullabies and rustled their leaves briskly to warn of an approaching storm. When it was time to travel, my mother would place my cradle board over the pommel of her saddle. I could watch the trees flashing by and smell the light aroma of grass bruised from the horses' hooves, and often I heard the song of the *cooxuceneihii,* meadowlarks, as they welcomed us among them.

I would like so much, Granddaughter, to speak to you of my childhood and the games we played. To tell you how I pretended I was the mother tending to my children, gathering wood at the riverside, breaking camp, and learning how to travel across the country carrying only the barest necessities. My friends and I would catch some of the camp dogs' puppies and try to get them to pull the little travois we built out of willow branches to imitate the migrating of our families. I would sit in a circle with my friends, giggling and chatting, pretending to work the hides and skins for tepees and clothing as we had seen our mothers and grandmothers do every day.

Grandmother, you knew, I think, even as a small child, that when you were older, preparing materials for the benefit of your family would be serious work, not only the tanning of hides but the decorating by quillwork and beadwork. Did you know, Grandmother, that our people became known for creating some of the most beautiful beadwork in Indian country? You will be happy to hear that the designs used in your day have been carried down through the generations, to be seen and treasured by many people— including my children, grandchildren, and great-grandchildren.

I've been told that at about age six your brothers would drift away from your mother and begin a learning time with their father, uncles, and male cousins who were, in the Indian way, their brothers. You would remain close to your mother and the other women in your camp. Each day was your school; each day was a part of the discipline of preparing for the life you would have among our people.

We have been told that you were nearly the same age as the man you married later in your life. I wonder if you knew him as a child or if you met him at a social gathering. It would be wonderful, Grandmother, to hear this part of your life story, a special time of romance and devotion. For these stories I would choose to sit with you by the river high in the mountains, surrounded by the lodgepole pines whispering in the wind. We could share the beautiful stories of male-female relationships, spiritually and physically joined to ensure the continuation of the Arapaho people.

Chapter Two

Grandmother, I believe all people have a memory or an awareness that recalls the first events in their lives. I have asked you about your first memories of life, and now I would like to share mine.

As a toddler I remember two shiny eyes staring at me as the flat gray head slithered over the top of the log cabin's doorsill. The step was made of soft pine, worn smooth in the middle by years of heavy traffic from boots, brogans, and my grandmother's soft tennis shoes. The gray patterned body slithered slowly into the room. The head moved purposefully back and forth, black tongue darting. This strange creature did not threaten me as it slid past, but instinctively I knew my grandmother should know about it. With the slow, determined steps of an eighteen-month-old child, I went to Grandmother Anna.

Grandmother Anna was washing the breakfast dishes. Grabbing her print dress, I pulled insistently trying to get her attention. She looked at me but kept washing the dishes. I jabbered to her in Arapaho, pointing to the cupboard where the creature had disappeared. Grandmother sighed, dried her hands on her apron, and reached down to me. I kicked my feet and pointed. Why wouldn't she look where I was pointing? As she started across

Anna (Hart) Ayers, maternal grandmother of author. Courtesy, Spotted Horse Collection.

the room with me, we heard a sharp rattling sound. Grandmother Anna stopped short, then tightened her hold on me and ran out the door. She yelled to my uncle Lester who was irrigating the garden by the cabin, "Hurry up! There's a snake in the house! It's in the cupboard. The baby must have seen it because she keeps pointing to the cupboard."

My uncle grabbed the shovel and raced into the house. Grandmother Anna, holding me close, followed him. He flipped open the bottom cupboard door. There was the creature coiled in a circle, its tail erect and rattling. Grandmother quickly carried me outside. Thus I was not a witness to the snake's demise. As I think back to that incident in our cabin at Lenore on Crow Creek, Grandmother Goes In Lodge, I believe the rattlesnake knew I was a baby and would not harm him, so he slithered by without bothering me.

Years later, when I was about six, the family was discussing how long it takes a rattlesnake to die. Ranchers in Owl Creek Valley said that if you hung a snake over a fence, it would not die until the sun went down. I thought of the day in the cabin at Lenore, and I asked my uncle, "Remember the snake that got into the house when I was little? Did you really kill it, and did it wait until the sun went down to die?"

My uncle looked at my grandmother in amazement. "When did you tell her about the snake?" Grandmother Anna said she had never mentioned the snake to me and had no idea that I would remember it. But I truly remembered the incident. And that, dear Grandmother Goes In Lodge, was the first day I remember of my life.

I never recalled anything earlier. This is probably good, as apparently the beginning was not particularly happy. I started life in a good way, born out on the prairie, much the same as you were. It was August, and my family was on the way to the reservation hospital at Fort Washakie when I announced my imminent arrival into this world. The wagon pulled off the road onto the flats near the hot springs. Camp was hastily made, and so my life began in the traditional Arapaho way.

I have no memory of living with my family—my father, Arlo (your grandson); my mother, Gertrude; sister Margaret; or brother Bill. No memory of hearing any discussions about the several siblings who were born and died before I entered the world. The 1920s on the reservation were not a good time to be born. Many babies died from malnutrition and from childhood diseases unknown before the white man came. Measles, scarlet fever, diphtheria, whooping cough, and pneumonia took them quickly when the Arapaho—weary, hungry, and malnourished—were first brought to the Wind River Reservation. They had no resistance to the white man's diseases and received limited medical care, in part because Arapahos were suspicious of the white man's medicine and were reluctant to seek assistance and in part because some needed medical services were not available. Tiny graves filled the Sacajawea cemetery at Fort Washakie as well as the small Indian family cemeteries.

My oldest brother, James Eugene, named after my mother's father, died from complications of measles at age six. In time, my father would have twenty-one children; only eight survived to adulthood. Of my white mother's six children, only three lived to maturity.

The years preceding my tenth birthday held both traumatic and good times. When I was still a baby, my parents divorced, and my mother took me to live with her parents. My older brother and sister were at the St. Michael's Mission boarding school, and they remained with our father. The boarding school experience was becoming a fixture not only on our reservation but all across Indian country. Starting in the late 1800s, an average of 70 percent of Indian youths were subjected to the deculturation efforts of the boarding schools. My siblings became a part of that movement, and I had little contact with them until we were adults.

Years later my mother's father, Grandfather Jim, told me of the rainy spring night when my father came home from work and discovered that my mother had run away. It was inevitable that an Indian man married to a white woman in the years following the treaty days would have many problems living on the reservation. These were years of intense prejudice against Indian people, and the ranchers and other local residents had little tolerance for mixed marriages. White women who married Indians were called "Injun lovers"; white men who married Indian women were referred to as "squaw men." Mixed marriages did not meet with the approval of some Arapaho people either, but my father's family welcomed my mother—a fourteen-year-old white girl—into their family. My white grandparents always spoke well of my father and his family. Love triumphed for several years, I am told, but my parents' use of alcohol began to cause problems in their marriage. One morning after a night of quarreling, my father left for work, and my mother took me to her parents' ranch at Lenore, about twenty-five miles away in the northern part of the reservation.

Grandfather Jim was worried about what my father might do, so he sat all night in the kitchen of the log cabin with a rifle in his lap, listening for the sounds of approaching hoofbeats over the driving rain. At daybreak my father rode into the yard, soaking wet. He had ridden all night across the reservation, stopping only to let the horse rest. As he rode into the yard, the dogs began to bark, and Grandfather Jim stepped into the yard with the rifle over his arm. "No need for the gun," my dad hollered. "Just wanted to make sure the baby's all right and you're gonna want her in your home." Grandfather Jim invited him in by the fire to warm up and dry his clothes. Grandmother Anna fixed breakfast.

My future was decided while they ate. I was to live in the white world with my grandparents and my mother's brother, Lester, and her sister, Jean; my father would keep my sister and brother on the reservation. This was the first of my many moves back and forth between the two cultures. I learned to tolerate the white culture because it was my growing-up environment, but my Arapaho ancestry took over at birth, and I never felt like anything but an Indian. During the fourteen years of assimilation into the white man's way of life, my mind, body, and spirit became more and more Arapaho. The resistance was evident in much of my behavior, and I believe my grandparents and Uncle Lester understood this and gave me an incredible amount of freedom. Meanwhile, my mother was free to make a new life. She returned to the white world and left her children behind.

Soon after I came to live with my mother's family, they purchased a ranch on the other side of the Wind River Mountains. We left the reservation to live in Owl Creek Valley west of Thermopolis. We traveled over Blonde Pass by wagon, using a dirt road that to this day is an adventure in

Ayers Ranch; from left to right, Gertrude (Ayers) Amos, mother of author, Lester H. Ayers, uncle of author, Jean (Ayers) Murdock, aunt of author. Courtesy, Spotted Horse Collection.

mountain switchback driving. In those days it was mostly two tracks, with many washouts that had to be filled in as you went. Grandmother Anna said she walked beside the wagon and carried me when the road was particularly rough. The wagon tipped over once, but the dining room table was the only casualty. Grandfather Jim repaired it, and we used it at the ranch for many years. Years after my grandparents died, I found the table in a garage in Hamilton Dome, Wyoming. I had it refinished and the legs shortened. It has been my coffee table for many years. It reminds me of my childhood among white people who respected my Arapaho heritage and understood my eventual return to the traditional ways of my people.

I know the spirits of my early family feel comfortable visiting wherever I might be. We have no material things to bond us, Grandmother Goes In Lodge, but we are bonded to one another as *Hinon'eino,* and our spirits are free to mingle. As I put these words into a white man's computer and print them on white man's paper, I hesitate. After all, we had only oral *hoo3itoono* (history stories) to pass on to others. The white man's words do not always give the true meaning of our thoughts, but my writing is meant in a good way. I think you understand how it brings me closer to you and to the knowledge I might have gained from you. So as I continue to write, it seems you may be laughing with me at some Indian story others would not understand or studying my intent and encouraging me. Then I am comfortable, and I continue.

My early years, Grandmother, were a time of learning, as were yours. My second and continuous memory of life begins after we had settled into the ranch house at Anchor, directly north of the Wind River Reservation. I lived there with my grandparents, Lester, and Jean. Aunt Jean was known in those days as a "change-of-life baby," born unexpectedly when my grandparents thought their parenting days were over. She was much younger than my mother and Uncle Lester but was several years older than me. She believed it was her lot in life to boss me around and make my life miserable. When I learned to break my own saddle horses, I was often thrown rudely to the ground. She hovered about waiting to yell to the world "And another redskin bites the dust!" We later became buddies, almost like sisters, but our relationship always had a competitive edge. I think, Grandmother, this was the case in part because she had a mother for a confidante and I did not.

Uncle Lester became my father figure; Grandfather Jim was more my partner in adventure. He was always game for doing unlikely things, and I was good at thinking them up. Grandmother Anna ran the family, which left Grandfather and me to march to our own drums. Grandmother Anna allowed no cursing or bad language in her presence, but when Grandfather was particularly agitated about something he would say, "This reminds me of my friend, whose name was 'Don't Give a Damn' Jones." He would stomp out of the house saying the name over and over. I was impressed. I thought this would be a good way for me to express my dissatisfaction with one of Grandmother Anna's orders. But when I tried it, Grandmother Anna said "Stop it! You don't know anybody named Don't Give a Damn Jones."

Grandfather Jim's family were conservative dairy farmers with solid reputations in New Jersey. He, however, loved adventure, and the West called to him early in his married life. He was known for wheeling and dealing. He considered it an exciting game to buy, sell, or trade almost anything. One day the family might be farming, the next day they were owners of a commercial business. His ventures were usually profitable, but there were occasional pitfalls. One of Grandmother Anna's favorite stories was of their life in Silverton, Colorado, where they owned a silver mine before deciding to move to the Wind River Reservation. Life with Grandfather, she said, could be summed up thus: when she woke up in the morning she never knew whether she had a maid or if she was the maid.

Grandfather Jim, with his love for adventure, was also my teacher. He taught me to handle with respect the guns associated with ranch life. The .22 was easy to learn, the rifle a little harder to master, but it was the shotguns that literally set me back on my heels. Grandfather Jim liked to go duck hunting, and the first time he let me shoot the twelve gauge he prepared me well. At eight years of age I was tall but slender. He told me, "Put the padded stock firmly against your shoulder, brace yourself, and when you are ready, fire." After picking myself up off the ground three times, I finally got the hang of it, and we spent many hours hunting on the creeks and lakes. He was always emphatic about guns. "Don't put a shell in the gun unless you are going to fire it," he said. "And don't pull the trigger unless you know what you are going to hit." In all our years of hunting we never wasted bullets, and we never had an accident. Coyotes, gophers, and other varmints destructive to the welfare of the ranch feared us; Grandmother Anna did not. She was not impressed with our hunting and refused to clean any of our game. She was also acutely aware of our ruses to avoid "real" work.

Uncle Lester was my mentor, Grandmother, and as he recognized the Indian traits so prominent in my behavior, he allowed my independence to grow. Uncle Lester was well built, over six feet tall, with curly, reddish-brown hair—indicative of his Scotch-Irish background. He had a pleasant manner that caused him to have many friends, including women.

Uncle Lester had an air of confidence and displayed extreme patience in the face of ranching hardships during the years following the Depression. I benefited from his forbearance. He taught me as the Indians did in your time: allow the child to learn by experience, without stifling her curiosity and her rush to know it all.

My lesson in survival began with a brown horse named Min. She was fat, spoiled, and just patient enough to become my greatest source of independence. Uncle Lester introduced me to Min when I was four. She was the first horse I was allowed to call my own. Uncle Lester's briefing on ownership dealt with responsibility. Until I was big enough to assume the physical care of the horse, I was to ride her only under his direction. Eventually, I would be responsible for all of her care. I was excited, but I understood this was a big step for me. I had always ridden perched in front of Uncle Lester while he guided the horse. Sitting on Min's broad back was not easy; my legs stuck straight out sideways as if I were doing the splits, and each time Min took a step I lurched to one side or the other. As my legs grew a little longer, Min and I began the struggle of determining who was boss. I would lead her to the fence and crawl up on it ready to hop onto her back—just as her rear end swung out of my reach. I appealed to Uncle Lester, who said, "To get along with horses, you have to be smarter than they are." He told me to try again, and as Min swung about he delivered a noisy whack on her rear with his jacket and yelled "Stop it!" That ended the problem. Uncle Lester explained that it is never acceptable to abuse an animal; the noise would be sufficient for the correction.

Until I was eight I rode Min bareback, just as my Arapaho ancestors had traveled over the prairies. Uncle Lester knew I would ride many miles from the ranch house, and he didn't want me to get tangled up in gear. As usual, he was right; I fell off many times and hit the ground free and clear.

By the time I was twelve I was helping Dare (one of the many young men to whom Uncle Lester gave a home) break all the horses on the ranch, both riding and driving. We had some exciting experiences, but I never saw any of our horses abused. I cannot say the same for the horses' behavior; they abused us plenty. I was thrown off in cactus, rocks, sagebrush, and creek bottoms; stepped on, rolled on, and smashed between their hairy bodies. But it was in my Indian blood to love the freedom riding horses gave me. It helped me develop independence and learn a sense of right and wrong, and it taught me to respect the four-leggeds and to appreciate their worth. My uncle never restricted my riding, never asked me where I was going or where

I had been. I saw what good care he took of the horses. Having my own horse, I believed the world was mine. Tell me, Grandmother, did you have a horse when you were small?

Granddaughter, when I was a young child every boy and girl was given a pony. It was not unusual for children to own several horses before they reached age twelve. The boys began to ride at three years of age and girls soon after. When a woman married, her husband would care for her horses but would never claim them as his own. I was an excellent rider at an early age. If the camp had to flee from an enemy at night, I was prepared to leap on my horse and follow the others to safety.

There was no formal school for me, but my lessons of life were taught every day within the extended family. I was taught the moral, mental, familial, and spiritual ways of our tribe. My cousins, considered brothers and sisters, had an important part in helping me learn by imitating in play the work of adults. I was encouraged to participate in adult activities. Children also participated in social gatherings. They took part in social dances, such as the Squaw Dance, the Owl Dance, the Rabbit Dance, the Wolf Dance, and the War Bonnet Dance.

Our people are courteous and friendly but reserved until friendship is established. Verbal greetings and shaking hands are traditional. Children were taught the importance of shaking hands at an early age; if they failed to do so, elders reminded them. Grandmothers and grandfathers talked to the children, telling us to be good and to listen to our parents. They would talk about what was right and wrong, and we were cautioned against bringing shame to our family through bad behavior. It was a wonderful way of learning among those who loved and cared for us. Continue, Granddaughter, telling me of your learning in the white man's school.

Grandmother, school for me in the white man's world became an experience in learning and discipline. When I was in elementary school, Owl Creek schools resembled many other country school systems in the western states. Each community had a one-room school where the imported schoolteacher lived (unless she was lucky enough to find a ranch family who provided room and board). The teachers usually came from back East and were at the mercy of country-wise ranch kids. It was a rough life for teachers in the mid-1900s, with no heat or electricity in the schools. Teachers had to build coal fires in the schoolhouse, often in −20° to −30° weather. Many teachers came west looking for husbands. Some were successful, but many ended up returning to "civilization."

For me, it was helpful that I had a good-looking, highly eligible bachelor uncle on the school board who never married any of the teachers despite their gallant efforts. I used this to my advantage a few times, but only in emergencies. Those emergencies were usually prompted by the fact that I was different from the other schoolchildren.

Grandmother Anna knew I would face cultural problems as I grew up because of my Indian heritage. She had experienced prejudice herself when her daughter was married to my father. While living on the reservation, she saw signs in the town cafés that read "No dogs or Indians allowed." She was aware of the discrimination both cultures exhibited toward "half-breeds" or "breeds." Having lived in Tennessee for several years, she had seen prejudice toward black people and chose not to let discrimination be a part of her life. But she wanted me to be prepared for the possibility that I would experience it.

Prior to attending school, freedom was important to me. Housework was not my favorite pastime. I preferred to trail along with my uncle outdoors, but Grandmother Anna occasionally put her foot down and told Uncle Lester to leave me in the house. She created all kinds of activities to help me learn social and housekeeping skills, which she considered vital to my education in meeting the challenges of becoming not only a woman but an Indian woman in a white man's world.

Dish drying was less boring when she brought out a huge dictionary, told me to close my eyes and point to a word, then to open my eyes and pronounce, spell, and give the definition of that word. For a five-year-old, I came up with some mighty strange words—*pax vobiscum* (peace be with you) in Latin, for example. I would use these brave new words whenever I was called on the carpet for some minor infraction. Uncle Lester would laugh, but Grandmother Anna was not impressed.

During the long winter nights, with the house locked up tight against blizzards and −30° weather outside, we read by the yellow light of an old kerosene lamp. Although a strict taskmaster, Grandmother always brought a special pleasure to reading—B. M. Bower's Flying U books, Zane Grey, and Charles Dickens—we enjoyed a wide variety of books. Years later I came to appreciate and understand why Grandmother Anna was so adamant about my learning to read.

My fifth birthday came in August, and in September, when Aunt Jean gathered her books and pencils for the beginning of the new term at Anchor school, I announced that I was also going to school to check it out. Perhaps I might like it and stay. Looks were exchanged among the family. Everybody laughed. Uncle Lester said, "Go; you will be back before recess." I endured the extra neck-and-ears scrubbing, and off I went. I did not go home at recess, and this was the beginning of my formal education in the white man's world, Grandmother. It led me down a rocky road that continues to take me more deeply into both cultures even as I, myself, have become an elder and a great-grandmother.

My first day at school was wonderful. When the teacher, Mrs. Nations, gave the six-year-olds the alphabet to learn, I raised my hand and asked to skip all that because I could already read. Mrs. Nations, a native of the valley, had a husband who was embroiled in a disagreement with my uncle over some cattle. Therefore, she was not impressed with my uncle or me. She took me to the front of the room and said, "Miss Amos, read the first page of this book." It was the famous Dick and Jane reader, and I sailed right through the pages until she finally said "Stop. Stop. We believe you!" What a rush it was to stand up there and read without hesitation. That was my first lesson in the power of preparedness.

It was ironic that although instructing Indians was not Mrs. Nations's priority, one of her relatives married an Indian from Oklahoma and moved to our valley in Wyoming. Their children enrolled in the Anchor school and became my good friends and allies.

A short time after my abrupt entry into school life, reality set in. I was less than impressive on the school grounds. I was an Indian. I was called every derogatory name the other kids could think of. During the summer the sun added a tan to my natural brown skin, so my skin was even more different from the other children's white skin.

At first I was puzzled by some of the children's behavior because when their families visited the ranch, we played together and no remarks were ever made. Such was the power of my uncle. In later years some of these same boys shook in their boots when they came to the house, trying to catch my eye, and my uncle frowned at them. But on the school grounds there were no restrictions on the names they hurled at me, and by the second year they began to seriously hurt my feelings. Finally, one day I went home crying to Grandmother, announcing that I had quit school and was never going back. The announcement did not shock Grandmother nearly as much as my crying did. She seldom saw me cry for any reason, so she sat me down and explained a lot of things. She told me I was different, but I had a wonderful heritage, an Indian ancestry that went back thousands of years. She said I should never be ashamed of who I was. Others who had no knowledge of their ancestry were jealous, and I should feel sorry for them. Then she told me how to handle the problem: "When they call you bad names and make fun of you, tell them nicely that you don't like it. If they do it again, tell them that it is wrong to treat people badly and to stop it. If they do it again, beat the hell out of them!"

I stopped crying and nearly fell off my chair. My Christian grandmother, who read the Bible every day, who had such ladylike ways, who wouldn't let anyone curse in her presence, was giving me this advice. This was when I learned how much my grandmother Anna loved me, even though she was never outwardly affectionate. I took her advice with great enthusiasm, suffered a few abrasions in the process, but ended up with some lifelong friends. School became a more pleasant experience. One year I won the county spelling contest, and the fact that I was the only Indian participant doubled my satisfaction. Contrary to Arapaho tradition, I was becoming competitive.

As I look back, two events stand out in my memories of my first decade. Grandmother Goes In Lodge, I know you would understand their significance. The first was my special relationship with Grandmother Anna's father, Mr. Hart. I never knew his first name, as he was never addressed by it. At that time I did not know about the Arapaho way of treating the aged with courtesy and respect. I had no one to teach me as you did. All your relatives considered it a duty to care for the older ones. You were told that when the elders go for water, you should help them; when they hunt for wood, you should take the time to go and help them. You were told to call old people "grandfather" and "grandmother" even when they were not related to you.

In 1936, under the Homestead Act, Uncle Lester and Grandfather Jim filed for two homesteads on lands adjunct to the ranch. About two miles from the main ranch house they built two log cabins, one on each side of the dividing line. We moved from the main ranch and lived on the new homesteads until 1938. Mr. Hart came to live with us during this time. I do not recall any discussion of his circumstances. He just arrived one day. I knew her mother had raised Grandmother Anna, since her parents were divorced—a "disgrace" in those days—and her father was never mentioned.

One of the homestead cabins had an extra room at one end, and that is where Mr. Hart lived. He rarely ate meals with the family, as the meals were prepared in the upper cabin some distance away. He had difficulty walking and used a cane. My first real awareness of his presence came when I was assigned the task of delivering his meals. Mr. Hart was a true gentleman. He arose early each morning and put on his suit—complete with vest, white shirt, and tie—which made him seem strange and intriguing to a girl in blue jeans and boots. He carefully polished his wonderful vest pocket watch, shined his shoes, and was ready for the day. He had a soft voice and always spoke gently and kindly to me. He spent each day in that small room with only his books.

One morning when I brought him his breakfast, I sat on his doorstep and watched the sun come up, reflecting the shades of dusky purple and blue on the snowcapped mountain that heralded another beautiful Wyoming day. Caught up in the wonder of it, I impulsively asked Mr. Hart if he would like to walk down to the creek and see the spring. His look of anticipation nearly broke my heart. I had a whole world of exciting things waiting for me to explore, and he had only one small room in a cabin. We took off across the prairie, Mr. Hart explaining that he had to be careful not to fall down; broken bones would make him more of a bother. I barely came to his waist, but I held his arm and we had a wonderful walk, examining the sagebrush, looking for meadowlark nests, and finding a variety of colorful rocks.

I will not forget the look of joy on his face as he stood over the creek bank, watching the spring water cascading downstream over the rocks and gravel beds. As we strolled back to his cabin, he said, "We certainly are a strange pair of orphans, aren't we?" It took me several years to understand what insight he had into my situation in life.

Shortly after this excursion I came to breakfast one morning to find Grandmother Anna crying, and she told me Mr. Hart had passed away. This was my first experience with human death. I ran down the hill screaming "No. No. Not yet!" Uncle Lester caught me at the cabin door and asked me not to go in. I was still jumping up and down and yelling, so he opened the door and let me in. Mr. Hart was lying on his bed, carefully dressed as usual, as if to meet the Creator, and his face looked relaxed and peaceful. Uncle Lester said, "You made a big difference with your company. Let him go home in peace." As I look back, I am happy that our Arapaho people hold so much respect for our elders. They have earned our respect in more ways than we will ever know.

The second event was also traumatic, both physically and psychologically. The area between our ranch fence and the schoolhouse was open country. One day in early fall, Aunt Jean and I were walking home, swinging our little syrup bucket lunch pails and happy with the world. Earlier that day we had watched the Mill Iron cowboys moving cattle past the schoolhouse, bringing them down from open range in the mountains.

We were over the hill and about halfway to our fence when we heard a noise and looked behind us. A big red Hereford cow was tearing down the hill and heading our way, tossing her head, revealing huge and destructive horns. She was blowing froth from her mouth as she ran, and her eyes were red with the whites showing all around. She was fighting mad and, as Uncle Lester would say, hell-bent on hurting somebody. Too late we realized she must have a new calf somewhere in the vicinity. Aunt Jean yelled "Run for the fence!" as if I needed prompting. I remember falling down and hitting my head on some sagebrush. My nose started to bleed. I managed to get up, but I stumbled again and again, rolling around in the dirt and brush. Aunt Jean had made it through the barbed-wire fence and was still yelling "Run!" Her shouts seemed to infuriate the cow even more.

I looked back, and the cow was getting so close I could feel her breath on my back. I heard more crashing sounds, and suddenly someone grabbed my pants at the waist and lifted me up, yelling "Grab for the saddle horn and hang on. We have to outrun this cow, or she'll gore my horse." I hung on to everything I could get my hands on, including the cowboy's leg, and we raced across the prairie. The cow finally dropped back, and we cut across to the ranch house.

Grandmother Anna and Uncle Lester were out in the yard when the cowboy set me down. They shook his hand, thanking him profusely. He said, "I just happened to be there. Range cows get pretty testy when they come out of the mountains with new calves. Glad to help." And he rode off. The cowboy was Ray, Grandmother, an Oklahoma Indian and the oldest son of the Oklahoma family who had just moved to our valley. Some good spirits were following me that day, as, Grandmother, I believe you know.

Chapter Three

What an exciting time it was for me, Granddaughter, as I began the second decade of my life. It was time to accept the change from childhood to the increased responsibility of becoming a young woman. Now I would make serious use of the hours of childhood play and remember the lessons learned from playing adult roles.

Only recently, my play had included gathering and storing chokecherries, squaw berries, wild haws, and currants. My friends and I laughed and chattered while preparing pemmican. It was fun to pound the dried meat fine and mix it with fat or bone marrow and crushed chokecherries. I carefully shaped the mash into small patties to dry for future use on the trail. When my father or uncles brought in deer or buffalo meat, I would get small pieces of the meat, slice it, dry it, and put it away in my toy parfleches. These were made as playthings but were painted like the real ones. My mother taught me to braid my own lariats. I used them to pack my belongings. Sometimes this one-inch rope was also used to pack firewood. When I was small I helped my mother pack firewood, but as I became a woman, I was not permitted to pack wood on my back, as it might weaken me for childbearing. It became the duty of older women.

Play activities introduced to me as a child would soon become serious tasks that would provide food for my own family. By now I had chosen a girlfriend who was special to me in many ways. With the wonderful freedom of camping in exciting places, my friend and I wandered over trails in the forest or along the river's edge looking for childhood treasures. We both had a tendency to be reckless, and we learned to suffer the results of such behavior with good humor. Grandmothers are cautious caretakers, but they recognized the value of the childhood adventures with my friend. Such friendships are made early in Indian life and last a lifetime.

My friend and I would turn the forked poles used for a variety of tasks, such as moving pots around the tepees, into imaginary horses. We even had small saddles with cruppers for play, like real ones. Each of us had doll cradles, which were beaded, and we also had beaded saddlebags. Our mothers made us buffalo-calf hide robes to play with. They were tanned with the hair on, just like real robes. Some were decorated with porcupine quills or painted with designs.

Breaking and setting up camp was a way of life on the prairie. When game became scarce in the area, it was time to move on. The horses quickly consumed the grass near the camp. The younger boys had to move them farther out several times a day to provide continuous grazing. Occasionally, the water supply would diminish, and we would move to another river site. Whenever camp broke for a move, I was responsible for taking care of my playthings, bundling them up, and seeing that they were properly placed on the travois. When settling in at a new location, I unpacked and placed them in their proper place in the tepee where I lived.

The practice of mimicking elders as I played in my small tepees, using the little skins of rabbits and squirrels for beds and floor mats, was a good rehearsal for the coming years of nurturing and taking care of family members. When I reached my teens, I gathered the tiny hide pouches, the little backrest made of three willows sewn together with sinew, the buffalo-horn spoons and elk teeth, and with my mother's help decided which young relative would make the best use of these gifts. It was time to put away my little dolls, stuffed with buffalo hair and grass and wrapped in blankets of soft deerskin. Instead of treating them as babies, I gave them the courtesy of treating them as adults—I never treated the dolls as babies because I was not even allowed to talk about babies. Further, the dolls were not considered male and female dolls or thought of in any immodest way, such as pretending they lived together. Modesty was an Arapaho custom, and it was respected in this manner. I learned to cherish my dolls as I played with them each day. Therefore, I kept some for a future daughter. Some were stored away with other mementos of childhood.

Playing games and learning about the work of mothers, aunties, and grandmothers every day gave me the confidence to ease into puberty. These changes were so natural that our people did not give them great attention. There were no menstrual huts and no special ceremony such as other tribes sometimes held in honor of a girl's reaching puberty. About two years before the onset of my menses I wore a belt around my waist, losing some of the freedom of my loose-fitting childhood apparel. Belts were decorated with beadwork or silver. My mother and grandmother took great pride in the beadwork designs, setting an example for the artistic work I would be expected to learn. The Arapahos were known among the tribes as traders; and at the gathering of the nations in summertime, Arapahos traded with the southern tribes for decorative silver, which was highly prized.

Attached to my belt was my navel bag along with a beaded knife case, beaded awl case, beaded bouncing ball, and a little turtle-shell rattle. My brother had found the small turtle shell and placed it on an anthill so the ants could clean it, leaving the loose inner bones to form the rattle. The knife case and the awl case depicted the training I had received in learning to use these tools. A wide belt replaced these articles, which were taken off when I entered puberty—except the navel bag—and passed on by my mother to my brother's child. I could have kept the navel bag if my mother or grandmother had approved, but it would not have been worn after I reached puberty.

Camps were made close to water, and when I went swimming in the nearby rivers or lakes I wore light clothing to conceal the changes taking place in my body. I was still allowed to play with boys, but only during the day. At sundown I was required to come inside. I could no longer play at night. I was to stay close to my mother, auntie, or grandmother. By the time my menstrual periods began, my mother and other close female relatives had given me instructions. I was told not to go to any area where someone was ill lest I cause the person's condition to deteriorate, and I was not to take part in any ceremonial practices during that time. I was aware of many changes taking place as I approached puberty, but my family life flowed along in its daily routine, and I never felt self-conscious or embarrassed.

Our people did not openly discuss the onset of menses, but if you and I were given the opportunity to visit about the differences in our puberty years, Granddaughter, I would laugh because I understand you might be embarrassed to tell me of your behavior at that time. I believe your aunt Jean, six years older than you, met the challenge with quiet poise, and there was little discussion between the two of you on the subject. When you awoke one chilly morning and discovered the occasion had arrived, you were highly indignant, yelling for your grandmother Anna. She came into the room as you stormed about, pacing the floor and exclaiming, "What is this nonsense? I have no time for this. How can I get on a horse and ride off with this going on? And what do you mean, once a month? Once a year is too much!" Your grandmother Anna, always fond of quoting the Bible—especially when dealing with your behavior—simply stated, "The good Lord never gives us more than we can bear, and this too shall pass." As she left the room she looked back and said "Good luck next month," smiled, and closed the door. Don't ask me, Granddaughter, how I know these things. You might be surprised to know how many times I was not far from your side.

I came to admire the dignity shown by Arapaho women and the respectful way they accepted life changes. From the start of my menses, my association with my brothers changed greatly, as I will explain. Since cousins are considered the same as brothers and sisters, the same restrictions applied to my male cousins.

As a child, physical fitness was stressed early. Our people encouraged good physical and mental health through play activities, mock battles, hunting games, and competitive sports. An exception was ceremonial events. They were sacred, and children could not even pretend to take part in them.

Games were teaching tools. Small boys and girls played games together, romping through the camp and across the prairies. Common among Arapaho children were games such as carrying one another upside down and swimming across the river on our backs with one foot sticking above the water with a ball of mud on the big toe, which represented a grandchild. You had to swim feet-first and swim straight across, regardless of the speed of the current. Then you would line up to see who could dive in and swim underwater the longest and farthest. There was no great concern about the natural state of our bodies, and I spent many happy hours in the rivers and lakes, swimming and bathing with other children. We teased one another and had magnificent quarrels over minor incidents—all forgiven as we trudged back to camp at suppertime.

But with the onset of puberty I began to treat my brother in a new way. I began to show him respect for the important roles he would play in my life. We no longer spoke to each other unless it was necessary, and then, when speaking to him, I used a quiet voice and kept my eyes downcast. My brother would play a role in arranging a marriage for me and would accept the responsibility of looking after me for the rest of my life. If my husband was away hunting or engaged in battle, my brother would be my protector, and he would make sure there was food in my camp. I no longer teased him or joked with him. I became even closer to my grandmother, and my brother might give her orders regarding my behavior. He took his responsibility for me very seriously, and I would be grateful to him in the years to come because of the security he provided.

It is so delightful, Granddaughter, to share this period of my life with you. Was I apprehensive about my changing role, or was I just content to live each day to the fullest? I believe the changes came about so naturally because I shared a close and loving relationship with my female relatives. The days moved forward happily.

Was I secretly a little proud of my changing looks? We are taught to be humble and not overly proud. But I remember thinking I liked some of the changes. The sharp, angular shape of my child-body became softer, and I was conscious of the beauty of my glossy black hair, which was growing long because it was never cut. I spent more time keeping it clean and shiny. I washed my hair in the river; the water was soft, and we had a special way of rubbing a little buffalo tallow into our hair after we rinsed it. There were also plants we could rub in our hair to give it a pleasant scent.

I learned how to paint streaks down my face and on my cheeks, forehead, and nose to signify pressure or significance. I was taught the meaning of our paints. Red paint was used in profusion in exciting times—during war or when one was in love—and was put on the face, hair, and body. Black paint was used after returning from war, signifying joy or rejoicing. A line painted from the mouth down to the chin indicated peace. Paint on the face, unless for ceremonial purposes, symbolized happiness. The paints were prepared in special ways for social purposes, war, and ceremonies. The clay was dug in the mountains, pounded into powder, and then moistened with fat. We were told the paint ways were given by the Creator. The paints protect us from the heat of the summer and the cold of winter. The paints give us good luck.

After my menses began I wore a wrapping (to'jehet) around my body similar to an apron, and I wore a blanket that could be pulled up to cover my eyes. My dress was longer, and I did not bare my arms. I gave strict attention to my mother and grandmother, and in the presence of other people I was quiet and respectful. As you understand the need for humor to bring more happiness to Arapaho people, you can also understand the special times when my close girlfriends from childhood and I would get together. While hunting berries, carrying water, or gathering wood, we would laugh and chatter—much as you did when you were younger—always keeping an eye out lest our mothers would think we were too loud and noticeable.

This is the age when I was instructed in the Bänuxta' wu, or Buffalo Dance. I learned about the woman pledger of the dance (the woman who puts up the dance), the building of the lodge, and the activities of the four-day dance. This was an important ceremonial event, and women of various classes and ranks influenced the different parts of the dance. I was excited to be old enough to take part in this event. The dance was discontinued around 1897.

Arapaho society was highly organized; and marriage, as you know it, or taking a mate was important and was considered a serious part of that society. It was not considered appropriate for men or women to remain single unless it was for the benefit of the tribe, such as if one took on the obligations of the Coyote Men who guarded the camp by keeping watch from the top of the surrounding hills. Pledged to celibacy, they proudly dedicated a period of time to protecting the tribe. They were mostly young men who were not yet married or men who had lost their families. The time served could be several months to a year, and it was determined by a war council based on immediate need.

As my time neared for courtship and marriage, events in the outside world were taking place that would greatly affect our people throughout my adult life and down through the lives of my children and grandchildren. During this time, as I traveled across the prairie with my people, I was unaware of the many things taking place elsewhere in the land. Take a moment, Granddaughter, and tell me of these events.

Grandmother, our elders and our history books tell us that the Plains tribes had already endured many smallpox epidemics. This disease was the primary cause of an estimated 90 percent decrease in the Indian population between 1492 and 1900. A new epidemic in 1837 eradicated the Mandan Indians, a Sioux tribe of 10,000 concentrated in nine villages along the Missouri Valley in North Dakota. Fewer than 100 Mandans survived the epidemic. Although smallpox had an impact on our Arapaho tribe, heavily at times, there is no knowledge of the exact numbers who were lost. We know only that smallpox was a disease not of our doing, not of our culture, but our people suffered greatly from it. We know from our elders that although we had enemies and we fought battles to protect our camps and our buffalo herds, we never inflicted death indiscriminately on women, children, and the innocent elders who had earned a peaceful old age. Smallpox did that. Moreover, to die in battle held honor, but there was no honor in a smallpox death.

To continue, Grandmother, it was also during the mid-1800s that within the white man's government the Indian Service was transferred from the War Department to the Interior Department. The Indian Service became more political and corrupt. Indian agents, appointed through congressional patronage, represented tribes incompetently in treaty negotiations. The corruption affected Arapaho people when the Fort Washakie Indian Agency was established in Wyoming. Your children and grandchildren would be treated condescendingly by this branch of the government for many years and under many trying circumstances.

Grandmother, our written history tells us how a pass discovered through the Rocky Mountains led to the opening of the Oregon Trail. Thousands of white settlers began to arrive in wagon trains, traveling across Indian country through Nebraska, Wyoming, and Idaho to reach Oregon. This added to the already strained relationship between the white people and the tribes. A few years later, after gold was discovered at Sutter's Creek in California Territory, tens of thousands of people from all over the world poured into the territory to make their fortunes. Waves of white people continued to push our people further and further from their nomadic life on the prairies.

Granddaughter, at this time I had little awareness of the future. I was busy preparing for my new life as a wife and mother. A husband was chosen for me. That husband was later killed, leaving me with two children. When I married the second time, I did not know the importance that husband would have on the welfare of the Arapaho people. I did not know how to prepare to be one of Chief Sharp Nose's four wives—Forest Woman, Water Snake, Buffalo Woman, and myself, all sisters. But I would learn to share the heavy responsibility of meeting the needs of a young chief, on whose shoulders rested many responsibilities of his own. He would fight, protect, negotiate over the years, and always try to clear a safe path to a good life for the people who cared for him as he cared for them. He was expected to do all of this against overwhelming odds. It would be a fight for survival, and I was there to stand beside him. I worked with my sisters as a team and was constantly prepared to protect the family from injury, starvation, and disease. Events were taking place that would not make my load lighter or easier to understand. All I wanted was the freedom of the prairie and the opportunity to raise my family the traditional Arapaho way. That was not going to happen.

Courtship could have been a simple progression of events, or it could have been worrisome. If I were to become the first wife of a warrior, courtship would follow a natural course. A tall, dashing young man might have caught my eye as he rode into camp, declaring victory over the enemy. Or I might have seen him going into the Chiefs' Council to meet with the men who planned the battle, then leading them out in full regalia to charge the enemy.

It was the custom for Arapaho mothers to strictly watch their daughters at all times. They even accompanied girls to the bushes when they went to attend to nature's demands. They watched closely for any young men seeking an opportunity to talk to their daughters. I was aware of my mother's caution as I prepared for my courtship days.

When I was old enough to have my own things, I had two beaded hide bags for my clothes that sat neatly beside my bed. My beaded saddle-packet bag hung on my willow bed. I learned to keep sweet-smelling leaves, packing them among my clothing, putting some in my pillow, and keeping a bunch tied in a small, gaily colored calico cloth on my necklace beads. I collected seeds from certain plants growing in marshy places, which when pounded fine would be dampened and used to perfume my clothes and hair. The case for my personal items was made of hide and was nicely beaded. It held my paints—mostly red and yellow—to paint my face, a stick to part my hair, and a porcupine-tail brush. Any jewelry given to me was also kept in this case and was available when I wanted to look my best, perhaps to impress the young men as I did my own private search for the one who would become my husband.

There were several ways a warrior might show interest in a young woman. When she went down the path to carry water, he might approach her with a greeting. It would need to be brief because of the watchful eyes of her female relatives. My mother continued to talk to me about my behavior and warned me not to respond to the flashes of the mirrors young men held at a distance, which indicated the young men's opinion of the girl's character. Even if a girl might be interested in the young man who flashed the mirror, she would not respond, as it was an improper way to approach an honorable relationship.

If I was attracted to someone who was also attracted to me, I could agree on a time when I would come out to adjust the tepee flaps to create more draft to remove smoke from inside. Smoke control within the tepee was a daily necessity and would not call attention to my meeting the young man. Each time we met and exchanged words, the relationship became stronger. This was a time of getting acquainted and deciding if this was to be my lifetime mate. If he was not my choice, I could avoid talking to him, and he would soon understand. But if the mutual interest intensified, it was understood that the next step might be for the man to engage his niece in a plan to have me over to visit her, and he might drop by. Most young girls enjoyed this innocent deception and were happy to assist their uncles in arranging the meetings.

The man who wanted to become my husband was required to talk with my oldest brother, Eagle's Head (or an uncle if I had no brother), and my parents to ask that I become his wife; he did this either in person or through female relatives. My brother could refuse, but even so, he would talk it over with my parents, older relatives, or my mother's brothers. My brother would then ask my mother or both parents to tell me about the man's wishes. I could refuse or accept his offer. Usually, I would follow my brother's wishes out of respect and the knowledge that he was acting in my best interest.

My potential husband might go hunting and have his parents deliver the meat to my family. They could then ask that I be his wife. Again, my brother would be the one to discuss the possibilities of marriage at this time.

Once I decided the man was the one for me, marriage plans would move quickly. There was no formal marriage ceremony, but in actuality the entire process was ceremonial, conducted following the traditional ways of the Arapaho people.

There would be a proper exchange of gifts between the two families. There was still time for me to reject my suitor, but at this point the relationship was fairly well established, and the exchange of gifts signified both families' pleasure.

My parents would provide the tepee for my new home. The new tepee, with the new couple residing in it, told the world of the marriage and was symbolic of the marriage itself. Late in the evening my mother would cook supper and invite my new husband's male friends and relatives to come and eat. After eating, they would have time together, visiting and smoking. Only then were other relatives invited to attend the feast. This usually took place at midnight. Often an elder or a medicine man was asked to speak and provide a blessing. Other elders would council my husband and me on how to get along, show respect to each other's families, and be thoughtful toward all members of the tribe in our new position as a married couple.

My first marriage was a traditional one. My husband was from another tribe, and for a time we traveled with his family. After our second daughter was born, he was killed in a hunting accident, and I returned to my tribe, the Arapaho. Because I was so young, my brothers accepted the responsibility of caring for the girls and me.

However, if I had not been the first wife and had come to the family as a second or any subsequent wife, the marriage process would have been very different. If a husband asked that a sister be added as a wife, the request was discussed with the brother and parents and was made known to the first wife. If she agreed—as she usually did out of respect for her husband and her family—the additional wife would either share the family tepee or be given her own tepee to live in. If another new wife—possibly another sister—was requested as a third or fourth wife, she would likely be asked to share a tepee with one of the earlier wives. She could decline the offer, but the family still made the decision, and she would abide by their wishes.

If I, as the first wife, had a married sister whose husband died or was killed, that sister would be added as a new wife, and my husband would take care of her and her children for the rest of their lives. As was the custom, the grandparents of the family actually took care of the children, leaving the wives to tend to the many camp duties and responsibilities.

The man destined to become my second husband was a striking man. He was five feet eleven inches tall and weighed nearly 200 pounds; he had broad shoulders, was muscular, and was bronzed and eagle-eyed with long black hair. He was a magnificent figure, handsome and self-assured. An army official, John A. Bourke, described Chief Sharp Nose in 1872:

> Sharp Nose of the Arapahos was tall, straight, of large frame, with piercing eyes, Roman nose, firm jaw and chin and a face inspiring confidence in his ability and determination. His manners were dignified and commanding, coming nearer to the Fenimore Cooper style of Indian than any I have seen. Sharp Nose, the Arapaho chief, with dilated nostrils and flashing eyes, moved nervously from point to point on his wiry pony, looking [like] the incarnation of the Spirit of War. (Bourke, "MacKenzie's Last Fight with Cheyennes: Awlute's Campaign in Wyoming and Montana" [New York: Military Service Institute, 1890].)

When the time came for me to know him better, I saw a young man who quickened my heartbeat, who stirred my very soul with longing and anticipation. Then came the important questions. Did he like me, and would he want me for his wife? Would my family, particularly my brother, approve?

Since my marriage to Chief Sharp Nose was my second marriage, the courtship was different from my first. I had children and could make my own choices, although I still respected my brother's wishes. The custom of family negotiations was still followed. This man who became my husband had been described by so many—white men, military men, and his own tribal members—that I must have recognized his potential when I first met him. I was very attracted to him personally, but I still respected that he was a great warrior; he was handsome, dignified, brave, and traditional in all ways.

As I became a member of this historic family, all according to custom, I had no doubts or misgivings about the future. I did not know that the traditional way of life was slowly fading and a different life was emerging—one in which my warrior husband would be removed from the battlefield

Chief Sharp Nose, c. 1877, in military dress. Courtesy, Spotted Horse Collec-
tion, source unknown.

and temporarily housed with the former enemy as a scout. How could I
have known that if he failed to cooperate, our pitiful band of Arapaho,
numbering fewer than a thousand, would be at greater risk and might dis-
appear into the gray nothingness of another culture?

What a dilemma I faced in the coming years. As the wife of a chief, I would travel with him across the country, never knowing where I would lodge each day. The days were much the same as I adjusted to my new married life. But at night, when people gathered around the fires, I heard more and more of the white man—*Nih'oo3oo,* or Spider—a creature capable of wondrous and mysterious things who could also be deadly.

This white man seemed strange to me—a man with lighter skin who lived in a manner quite different from the natural camp life I enjoyed. You asked, when I first saw the military man, whether he was frightening with his strange uniform and shiny regalia, his horses thundering into the village, bridles and stirrups shattering the quiet of the camp. And did I consider him a threat to my future and to the futures of my children, grandchildren, and great-grandchildren—including you. I cannot say; the war was men's business, and women were reluctant to discuss war parties and their purpose. The treaty days were soon to come, and with them came some of the greatest challenges my young husband and I would face in our life together.

Chapter Four

Grandmother, my childhood years passed quickly, shifting from here to there with each crisis significant enough to remember. It is sometimes said that the good, the bad, and the indifferent can measure one's whole life. My path to puberty seemed to include all of the above. The good part was I had a home, nobody beat me, life was interesting, and I was physically and mentally healthy. The bad would ebb and flow like the tides.

By age six I quit going up into the attic and sitting by the dormer window to cry for my mother and wish for a home with two parents like those of my neighborhood friends. I spent too much time staring down the road that led out of the valley to the rest of the world, of which I knew very little. Somewhere in that unknown space lived my mother with her husband, Harold; and except for her fleeting visits home once or twice a year, she was not a part of my life.

One day I dried my tears, kicked the trunk that held my mother's cast-off clothes, and stomped down the stairs. I found Uncle Lester in the living room reading the paper. Standing with chin jutted out and hands gripped behind my back, I announced, "I hate my mother, and I hope she never comes to visit us again." He looked at me for a moment and patiently laid the paper aside.

Gertrude (Ayers) Amos, mother of author. Courtesy, Spotted Horse Collection.

"You're pretty young to be discussing this," he said, "but you should never hate your mother. You can blame me if you want. When your mother and father decided they could not live together anymore and brought you to our house, I talked to your mother. I told her I would adopt you, take care of you, and educate you and that you would never be cold or hungry or without a home. In return, she was never to come after you to drag you around from pillar to post—no matter what." He continued firmly, "I meant it. She was a divorced woman with no job skills, and she had a bad habit of drinking too much on occasions. She was free to live her life however she wanted, but she was to leave you in this home until you were eighteen. She was welcome to come and visit you at any time, and she has done this over the years. So if you want to hate anyone, feel free to jump on me, but I will always treat you like a daughter. Okay?"

I thought about all this for a while, then I said, "All right, Uncle Lester. Thank you for telling me. Forget my mother." That was the last time I ever shed tears over being separated from my mother. I didn't even cry at her funeral six years later.

During this time I was indifferent toward my father. I felt no sense of loss and had no memory of him. Grandmother Anna would sometimes speak of him, always in a good way. She often talked about the Arapaho people, especially the women who had become her friends when she and Grandfather lived on the reservation. She stressed the fact that I was Indian because of my father, a full-blooded Arapaho, and that I should be proud of my heritage, a very special one dating back centuries. Only in later years did I learn to appreciate her attitude toward the Indian people and how valuable it was to me growing up.

Grandmother Goes In Lodge, when did I realize I was Arapaho, an Indian? That is a question you would never have understood or asked. You were born into an Arapaho family in the Arapaho Tribe, and you knew no other way. You were fortunate to come into this world knowing who you were and accepting yourself as a true gift of the Creator, as was the way of our people. As I grew into awareness of the world around me, I saw only white people, my friends and relatives on the north side of the Owl Creek

Mountains that separated our valley from the reservation. I did not feel like one of those white people.

All this changed the day Uncle Lester took me on my first trip back to the reservation to visit my dad and his family. I was excited about going with Uncle Lester. I must confess I was more excited about taking a trip through Wind River Canyon all the way to the reservation than I was about meeting my father, brother, and sister.

When I met my father, Arlo, for the first time, it was strange shaking hands with him. He was polite and treated me like a grown-up. He had an infectious smile as he looked me over and said he was glad we had come to visit.

I remember staring at him curiously and seeing a nice-looking man wearing sunglasses, Levis, and cowboy boots and hat. His black hair was short, and he had an outgoing personality that put me at ease. I immediately liked seeing this person who had the same dark skin as I and who showed confidence and pride in his appearance.

My father introduced me to his father, my Grandfather Rex. My Grandmother Caroline, your daughter and Rex's wife, had passed away in 1931. Grandfather Rex was magnificent, very regal in appearance. He was tall and slender, with long white hair in tiny braids, a large black hat, Levi's, and full-beaded moccasins. As we shook hands, he spoke to me in Arapaho. In fact, he never spoke a word of English to me during any of our visits. Grandfather Rex lived in a tent, and I was told later about the modern frame house Dad had built for him. He walked through the house, thanked my father for the nice "box" to keep his things in, and went right back to living in the tent. On the day of our visit, Dad told me my grandfather wanted me to see his dog—who would not respond to English commands but who obeyed instantly when spoken to in Arapaho. Grandfather Rex spoke to the dog in Arapaho, and it sat. I told the dog to sit in English, and it gave me a doggy sneer and stared off into space. I was delighted.

We visited for some time, my father and grandfather both talking to me in Arapaho. I listened closely. They accompanied their speech with sign language, which helped me to feel more in touch with the conversation, although I had no idea what they were actually saying. I loved being there

Arlo Amos, Indian name, Spotted Horse, full-blooded Northern Arapaho, father of the author, c. 1935. Courtesy, Spotted Horse Collection.

alone with them and felt right at home. Dad explained in English that the few words I spoke when I left his home as a very young child were in Arapaho.

I recall little about those visits, Grandmother Goes In Lodge, possibly because I was only six. My most vivid impression was of the Arapaho women. They wore scarves over their heads, long print dresses, and buckskin moccasins that were sometimes beaded. Many wore plain moccasins with buckskin leggings that covered their tan cotton stockings.

Uncle Lester introduced me to many women, apparently former friends of my mother's, and they offered their hands in the soft handshakes common among Indian people. Their faces were wreathed in smiles. They hugged me and looked me over as they patted me on the head. In English they said over and over, "Ah, ah, Gertrude's baby, Gertrude's baby."

I did not see my sister, Margaret, or my brother, Bill, during my first visit. Margaret was the oldest child in the family and lived and went to school at St. Michael's Mission in Ethete, Wyoming. Brother Bill was the next oldest, and he also lived at the mission during the school year.

We usually visited the reservation during the powwow season, when families gathered to take part in the celebration. Uncle Lester would put our chairs around the edge of the dance arena, and he visited with each person who came over to speak. Later, I realized that for a white man he had many friends among the Arapaho and the Shoshone people.

Years later, Grandmother Anna told me about the time he had spent on the reservation and the many friends he'd made. Apparently, he and a young Arapaho woman had fallen in love. Because of discrimination against Indians and whites who intermarried, he decided not to put her through the hardships he saw my mother subjected to when she married my Arapaho father.

Uncle Lester never married, but the woman he loved eventually gave in to family pressure and married an Arapaho. She and my uncle remained good friends, and in later years we sat with her and her family at the powwows. I believe this was when I learned the meaning of respect. I had been told in the past: respect your Grandmother Anna's privacy; respect your aunt Jean's right to visit with her boyfriends without you lurking around. This was different; I saw total respect in action as I watched Uncle Lester and the woman he had loved visiting and laughing together. He respected their friendship, their past relationship, and her present family. Happy to be with her, he asked for nothing in return other than her respect and friendship.

My uncle was not prone to discuss personal matters. Years later, in one of my bursts of reckless behavior, I asked him why he hadn't married her and lived happily ever after. He looked at me for a long time. Finally, he told me that later in life I might understand that all he had to offer her was a lifetime of hard work on a ranch. She would be separated from her people and her culture. Other ranchers and their wives would discriminate against her because she was different. He wanted a better life for her, he said. With a smile he added, "Besides, I have enough women in this household bossing me around."

Grandmother, I think you will understand why the Indian women intrigued me from my first visit. Even though they were strangers and different from the people of the valley in which I lived, there was a familiarity about them. The clean, dusky, earthy smell when they hugged me, the sincerity and warmth of their touch, promoted special feelings that had been suppressed by the separation from my mother. It wasn't that I didn't love Grandmother Anna. She treated me fairly, and I knew she loved me in her own way; but she was never demonstrative, and there was always a certain restraint between us. That restraint probably came from me as much as from her.

In a later visit I briefly saw my brother, Bill. He was a good-looking young man, with a beautiful smile that lit up his whole face. I did not see him again until after World War II when he was close to death from tuberculosis contracted during his time in the army. I saw my sister once at the mission school. Margaret later went to Casper to stay with our mother and to attend high school. She and one of her friends ran away one summer and came out to the ranch. She made one or two other visits to the ranch while I was growing up, but our relationship as sisters did not develop until we had both been married for almost twenty years.

My sister's visits to the ranch were not always enjoyable. She and Aunt Jean were closer in age than she and I were, and they loved to terrorize me. Margaret was excited about city life; and she, her friend, and Aunt Jean decided to improve my life by giving me a bob haircut that was supposedly all the rage. My hair flew off amid their "oohs" and "ahs" about how good it looked. My sister stepped back to admire her work, and as she examined the back of my head she said, "How cute it looks. Just like a boy's behind"— meaning, of course, that in the back it looked like a boy's haircut. In my young mind I interpreted the words literally, and I went screaming into the yard: "Uncle Lester! Grandmother! I don't want my head to look like a boy's behind!" Two days later even I had to laugh about it.

Grandmother, our childhood days were very different, but we did have one thing in common. They were learning years for both of us. You adapted to a life on the prairie, one of the rigors of camp life and following the seasons. My childhood days on the ranch were significant in many ways. I remember that each day held new excitement.

I truly disliked mulligan stew, but because we had bands of sheep, mutton was a fact of life. Coming home from school, I would be starving and asking for food the minute Aunt Jean and I entered the house. Grandmother Anna would say, "There's hot mulligan stew on the back of the stove." I would say, "No, no, a thousand times no. I want some good food."

"You must not be very hungry," Grandmother would say. "Put your coat back on and do the chores." The chores consisted of gathering eggs, feeding chickens, and packing in wood and kindling to fill the box by the kitchen range. By the time I finished the chores, cold and still hungry, I would scarf down a big bowl of mulligan stew without comment and still be ready for supper that evening.

One winter evening it was –20°F, and Grandfather Jim met me coming to the house with my last load of kindling. He took one look at me and made me throw down the wood. He grabbed me and started rubbing my cheeks with snow, mumbling, "Crazy kid, don't you ever feel the cold?" Oh, I felt it all right, but I had no idea when the freezing level was reached. I ate my stew that evening with my face wrapped in cold towels.

I remember two other times when I was thrown in the snow after walking home from school and I had to suffer the indignity of the cold towel wrap. Frostbite can occur easily when the temperature is –20 and your face is exposed to the wind. Apparently, at that time it was thought that rubbing the affected parts with snow would draw the frostbite out, and cold towels would help restore circulation.

As much as I detested mulligan stew, I believe I disliked the sheep even more. In the early 1940s the family moved into the cabins on the homestead west of the main ranch, planning to run a band of sheep until we had "proved up" on the land. This meant we had to establish residence on the land for a designated time and make certain improvements, such as adding buildings and corrals. Then we planned to sell the sheep and run only cattle. That was our pie in the sky: cattle. I think everybody detested the sheep because of their constant need for attention.

James E. Ayers, maternal grandfather of author. Courtesy, Spotted Horse Collection.

As soon as the sun came up, Aunt Jean and I would have to take the dog, Bob, and follow the sheep out onto the prairie. We could go three different directions, so the walk was never boring. I hated to admit it, but some mornings were wonderful. The early morning dew on the sagebrush smelled fresh and pleasant. The mountains were never the same, changing colors in a variety of blues, greens, and deep purples depending on the weather and the clouds. Still, following sheep was monotonous, and that is what we disliked most. Aunt Jean would often take a book, walk to the top of a hill where she could see all the sheep, and sit down to read.

I loved to explore, and, Grandmother, this became my time to learn about our bird and animal friends. I knew which rocks held the little black-striped chipmunks, and often, as I gave them a few crumbs from the break-fast table, they let me watch their daily routines. I did not then know the special Arapaho relationship to meadowlarks, but one day I sat quietly as they built their nest in a clump of sagebrush. I would often stop and visit them. They allowed me to look into their nest at the beautiful little blue eggs, speckled with rust. One day two baby larks were nestled among tiny pieces of broken shells. Their little bodies were amazing to me—naked of feathers, the internal organs lined with blood vessels clearly apparent to the eye. If I made any noise, their little beaks would fly open, expecting food to be dropped in by their mother.

Granddaughter, I wish I could have been there to tell you about the Arapaho people's special beliefs regarding the meadowlarks. When an Arapaho child's top head bones are beginning to harden and he or she is just old enough to talk, the child is fed the cooked meat and boiled eggs of a meadowlark. The maternal uncle hunts the bird, but the child's mother cooks it and feeds it to the child. The belief is that a child so fed will talk early and have knowledge of things. It is believed that meadowlarks speak Arapaho. They say, "Some-body is coming" or "Go, cook."

Thank you, Grandmother, for sharing that with me. Another thing I learned as a child on the ranch was to keep a stick in my hand and make plenty of noise when walking across the prairie through the sagebrush because of rattle-snakes. I had many dangerous encounters with these reptiles as I grew up, and they certainly had my respect. I was told they wouldn't harm you if you stayed back and gave them time to get out of your way. It was not unusual to see them reach five feet in length. When they are longer than you are tall, you tend to keep out of their way.

One sunny morning Aunt Jean and I were cleaning chicken fryers down by the edge of the alfalfa field. We were sitting on an old mowing machine in the fence corner when we saw a big rattlesnake coming toward us. Aunt Jean yelled, "Kill it. Kill it quick. We can't get out of this corner." I was only six, and she was much bigger than I, but all she could do was let out blood-curdling screams. I grabbed a shovel that was leaning against the fence and smashed it down on the middle of the snake. He wriggled loose, and Aunt Jean yelled again, "Look out, he is climbing up the shovel handle." I shook him off and quickly chopped off his head. I don't remember being frightened, but I would have preferred that he hadn't come after us in the first place.

Following sheep around during the summer was a solitary learning experience, Grandmother. There was no one to explain about the plants and flowers, all the little animals scurrying over the ground, and other interesting marvels of nature. I could only learn by observing. You were so fortunate, Grandmother, when you lived close to this natural world. Your immediate and extended families were close by to answer your questions about Mother Earth. You were even taught early in life about special hunting ceremonies that would bring the animals close when food was needed.

Grandmother, I was around eight when I learned about electricity and thunderstorms. The storms came up quickly out of the southwest, sweeping over the mountains and down over the valley, bringing brilliant zaps of lightning and thunderclaps that shook the ground. One summer another rancher asked us to help bring a herd of cattle down from the mountains. We rode across the North Fork of Owl Creek and were heading across the flats when a dark cloud warned of an approaching storm. It was hot and dusty. Uncle Lester said to me, "There's a bad electrical storm coming. Tie your reins and loop them over the saddle horn. Put your slicker on, and jam your hands in your pockets and leave them there. Don't touch your saddle horn. Kick your feet out of the stirrups. Guide your horse with your knees, stay close to the cattle, and keep them moving. And don't touch your horse with your hands for any reason."

It was a bad storm. Lightning kicked up patches of dust all around us. With each clap of thunder, the animals became more restless. Just before the rains hit, small balls of blue and red fire moved between the horns of the cattle. I was so fascinated by all that was going on around me that I wasn't afraid. Later, when lightning killed one of my uncle's friends, I understood the significance of Uncle Lester's warnings.

Bringing the sheep herds in for shearing could be exciting. A group of Basque shearers made the rounds in our valley. In those days, with no electricity, they used old-fashioned clip shears. They grabbed a sheep, sat it up on its haunches, wrapped their arms around it, and quickly clipped rows across the sheep's stomach and back and around its legs. They were fast. When they finished, one whole fleece would roll off into a bundle to be tied. The wool sacks were long and were fastened in a high square rack with slats nailed to the frame to make a ladder to the top. It was my job to tamp the fleeces down into the sack until it was round and full. Jumping up and down on greasy sheep fleeces did little for my personal hygiene, but the lanolin worked wonders for my hair.

The hard work of spring lambing was Grandfather Jim's responsibility. Uncle Lester built indoor stalls and hauled feed and water. When lambing time was under way, the nights were my special time. Every three hours Grandfather would wake me up, and I would pull on heavy clothes and follow him out to the sheds. We walked through the corral looking for mother ewes in trouble. The quiet nights were cold and frosty. Warm air drifted up from the animals' bodies. As we moved through the low murmur of sheep breathing and grunting, they shifted around and pushed against our legs. If a ewe had given birth to her lamb, we would move them inside to "mother up," but if we found one having problems, we would stay with her until Grandfather had the lamb up and suckling. When we finished, we would return to the house, sleep for three hours, and go back again. Those were special times with Grandfather Jim. We walked around with our lantern during the night, talking softly. He would tell me how much I helped him. I was too small at the time to be of much physical help, and I probably asked too many questions, but those nights remain a wonderful memory of how special he was to me.

As I grew older I would hear the family discussing financial problems. Although we all despised running sheep, times were hard, and sheep brought in two incomes a year. Wool prices were fairly good each spring, and with the wethers we sold in the fall, bank payments could be made. Every month we would butcher a wether, wrap the carcass in cloth, and meet the stage on its way back to town.

In the early days we always called the mailman the "stage." I suppose the term dated back to when the mail was delivered by stage drivers. The ranchers continued to use the word. Later, I think, he became the mailman. We called him other names when he failed to come or kept us waiting at the mailbox for hours when we had mail we wanted to give him. Grandfather Jim had some good ones. Fortunately, Grandmother Anna never heard them. The mailman drove a pickup. From the ranch house, we looked down the lane to watch for him to come up the main valley road. On the days he delivered mail, there was great anticipation as to whether he would stop at our mailbox and bring word from the outside world or sail past us and proceed on down the road.

The driver would deliver our wether carcass to the grocery store with a list of our needs for the month. On his return he would bring us the groceries. Aunt Jean and I were always excited about getting "real" groceries. There would be the basics—flour, sugar, and salt. If things were going well on the ranch, we might get bacon, store-bought bread, a few canned goods, and maybe a small bag of candy. There was no exchange of money, so we sent only for necessities. The rest of our food came from the ranch.

We would catch a ride to town with the mailman when someone needed to go to Thermopolis on business, uusually to visit the bank or the doctor. We didn't get a car until Aunt Jean graduated from college and started teaching school. Until then, we only had a pickup for ranch work.

I don't believe money ever concerned me. I knew we were "poor," and we hardly ever saw money—maybe a dollar or two when Uncle Lester paid bills in town. We had a home, food, clothing, and the necessities of life. The family talked about how poor we were, but it didn't mean anything to me. My basic needs were always met. As I grew older, however,

I began to resent that other people out in the "world" had things we did not.

Christmas was a difficult time. We received catalogs in the mail that showed beautiful gifts and toys. The catalogs had a dual purpose. Buying toilet paper was unheard of during those days. The old catalogs were used in the little outhouse as soon as new ones arrived. The Montgomery Ward and Sears and Roebuck catalogs also helped us pass the time after dinner.

When we ordered from the catalogs, it was to get coats, shirts, and other clothing we had to have. One Christmas, during a particularly cold winter, Aunt Jean and I each got an orange, an apple, and one pair of mittens. Grandmother Anna made us flannel shirts, and we thought they were warm and wonderful. We never realized at the time that our grandparents and Lester received no presents. But Grandmother cooked a big goose, with dressing, fluffy mashed potatoes laced with real butter and cream, giblet gravy, home-canned vegetables from our summer garden, "homemade" cranberry sauce, and carrot sticks from the cellar. Her mince pies and pumpkin pies with whipped cream were tasty. We were happy.

The outside world reached us through two newspapers, the *Thermopolis Independent Record* and the *Casper Star Tribune*. My grandparents bought a radio. We had no electricity, so we used a battery. What a disappointment it was when the battery started to wear down. We knew it would take real money to get another one. My grandparents insisted that we listen to the news three times a day for ten minutes each time, and then we had to turn the radio off. Occasionally, they let us listen to a couple of shows in the evening, but the dark cloud of the threat of a dead battery hovered constantly over our listening time. I think about this now when it seems every house has several television sets on constantly with nobody listening.

As I say, Grandmother Goes In Lodge, poverty did not concern me much in those days, but the cold did. I grew to hate the winters. We had two stoves in the entire house. One was the kitchen range with a big oven and a water reservoir attached to the side. There was another heating stove in the living room where my aunt and I slept on a big bed in the corner. There was no heat in the two bedrooms where my grandparents and uncle slept. The stoves burned wood or coal, but it was years before we could afford to buy coal. As soon as the wood fires went out, at –30 or –40°F, the house got really cold. My aunt and I would put "sad irons" in the oven after supper. Before we went to bed, we wrapped the irons in towels and slid them under big heavy quilts to try to warm a spot large enough to keep us from freezing during the night.

Grandmother Anna was the first one up every morning. She built the fire in the kitchen stove. I don't remember ever getting up when she didn't have a breakfast of hotcakes, meat, and eggs ready for us. She would call me, and I would rush to the kitchen with my clothes, open the oven door, and try to thaw out both my clothes and myself as I dressed. The washbasin would be frozen solid, as was the water bucket. By the time breakfast was ready, the water in the reservoir was warm enough to wash with.

Forty years later I was in Arizona, and I was lying by the pool in the sun. A local came by and said, "Don't you know it is 105 degrees?" I said, "I grew up in Wyoming, and I am just now thawing out." The local laughed. But believe me, Grandmother, the winters were no laughing matter to me.

Grandmother, I have often wondered how you survived those winters out on the prairie, especially during times of war. I know the tepees are warm when you have the small fire in the center, but when you had to flee for your safety and move camp in the winter, it must have been very difficult.

Moving during the winter was difficult, Granddaughter. Before the threat of the white man, we had our own winter camps. The Chiefs' Council chose camping places. We often used the same spot year after year, as long as the game was plentiful. We had "weather prophets," men who had medicine to forecast weather. They could tell by the color of the clouds what kind of weather to expect. Hail clouds are white, rain clouds are black, and snow clouds are grayish-white. The weather prophets also watched the animals. When horses chased one another around in a circle or if they stampeded, a snowstorm was on the way, and we could prepare for cold weather. Much weather forecasting was based on common sense, animal behavior, and past events. To foretell more specific weather conditions, the weather prophet would have to conduct a special ceremony.

*Thank you, Grandmother. Even today with modern technology, weather fore-*casting in the white man's world is based largely on weather statistics from the past, similar to the way our Indian ancestors forecast weather.

I was becoming a teenager, and my uncle teased me about becoming a rancher's wife. He would ask which local boy would be the lucky one I would marry. That was never my plan. There was a big hill in front of the ranch house. I often went to the top of that hill and looked in all four directions, wishing I could see the world. I wanted to travel to all the far-off places Grandmother Anna talked about. And I wanted no husband to hold me back. I needed freedom.

I turned thirteen the August before I started high school. That was when I discovered that boys might be more than just pests. Until that summer I had not been interested in romance. Aunt Jean was dating, and I thought she acted so goofy that I teased her and laughed at her behavior.

So far, my only romantic episode had happened in first grade, and it ended in disaster. Glen, who was also in the first grade, was walking home with me after school. His brother and sister rode the horse down the road. We cut over the hill, having a good time badmouthing the teacher and the school in general. When we got to my gate where his siblings would pick him up, he leaned over to kiss me on the cheek. I was stunned. How dare he do such a thing! My reflexes were good, and my first reaction was to swing my lunch bucket at him. Unfortunately, my aim was also good, and my lunch bucket hit his head. Even small head wounds bleed profusely, and this was no exception. He started yelling. The blood really scared me. His brother, Bud, came along and started yelling, "You've killed my brother. Shame on you!" We stopped the bleeding by pressing a handkerchief against the wound, and his brother took him home. When I got home I told Grandmother I would have to quit school, and she would probably be having a visit from Glen's mother. She made me tell her what had happened. As she held my head against her ample bosom to stop my crying, I felt her shaking with laughter.

Until I was thirteen, boys were just people to ride calves with, to have races and roping contests with, to tolerate when they acted smart during branding, and to generally ignore. Then along came Floyd.

It was a warm, sunny afternoon, and I had been riding fence looking for the hole one of our heifers kept getting through. As I came into a little glen between the hills, I saw Floyd practicing with a loop in his rope. I had known him for several years, but even though he was a good-looking boy, I had never paid much attention to him.

Floyd had water tied on behind his saddle, and he offered me a drink. We sat there in the sun visiting. I asked how his roping was going. He said not very well. His dad had told him to stop roping the calves. He asked me to run by him and let him try to rope me. He made a couple of good catches. Once when I ran by, he caught me, jumped off his horse, and started drawing me in toward him. When I got close, he put his arms around me and kissed me gently but firmly on the mouth. Grandmother, I think I skipped pre-puberty, adolescence, and several other stages of life and moved right into adulthood. We were both embarrassed about the whole thing, but later we hung out together and went to dances. Then he enlisted in the service, and I kissed him goodbye as he waited for his ride to town. I never saw him again. He was killed during the war. All I had left were faded letters and sweet memories of my first kiss.

But now I knew boys could be important. Did I want to get married? No, I wanted to travel. Aunt Jean was going to college at Laramie, and in two years she would have her teaching degree. I was starting high school that fall in Thermopolis, and I was already convinced I wouldn't like it. I was right. Because of the distance, I had to stay in town. The couple I boarded with were elderly. They were nice to me, but school was not a good situation. My clothes were not like those of the fancy town kids, and I could hear them whisper that I was an "Indian." There were 300 students and only two Indian girls. I felt awkward and out of place, and most of all I missed the freedom of the ranch. I suffered through the first semester.

Once a month on a Friday I would take the school bus up the valley to the ranch and spend the weekend. One Friday night when I got on the bus to go home, one of the white girls from Missouri Flats told me to go to the back of the bus, and she and her friends all began to laugh. I knew what she was insinuating. I calmly said that I would sit where I pleased. As I started to sit down about halfway down the bus, she stood up—encouraged by her friends—and made another cutting remark about my sitting in the back. No one else on the bus had said anything, and they all watched closely as I walked down the aisle to where she stood. I grabbed her by the hair, threw her into the aisle, and told her what a rude and ignorant person she was while I banged her head on the floor. I expected the bus driver to stop the bus and stop the fight. He just kept driving. After pummeling her severely, I slammed her into her seat and walked back to my seat. Nobody on the bus moved or spoke. She screamed and cried until the bus stopped and she got off with her friends. When I got off the bus at the ranch, the bus driver said, "She had that coming. I figured you could handle it, and you did." I told my family about the incident, and they were unhappy about the obvious discrimination. They did not approve of my fighting, but they understood my reactions. The rest of my bus rides were uneventful, with seating a matter of choice. Most of the kids became friendly after that incident, except a few from Missouri Flats.

I did make friends in that high school, but there was always the feeling of not belonging, of being different and not quite fitting in with the groups that form among teenagers. I met some Indian kids who lived in town but didn't go to school. I started spending time with them and staying overnight at their house instead of going to school. The family I was boarding with told my uncle. One day he came after me and said, "If you are not going to go to school, you can at least help out at home." I think he was disappointed in my behavior, but I believe he also understood the difficulty I experienced with prejudice because I was an Indian. That semester ended my formal high school education in a white school. The next year I attended an Indian boarding school.

Chapter Five

Granddaughter, it was going to be a beautiful day on the prairie. Dawn was breaking over the eastern horizon as I stepped out of my new marriage tepee. This was my second marriage, but that did not make it any less exciting, and I faced the future with great hopes for my family. Facing east, I began my morning prayers. The glow of the sun beneath the horizon painted the prairie a glowing crimson blush of color. I had much to thank the Creator for—good health for my people, a loving family, and the people's blessing for my new marriage. A new husband whom I loved and respected had been brought to me in the traditional manner.

Smoke was drifting skyward over the camp as women stirred the coals of last night's fire and began building a new cooking fire to prepare breakfast. Occasionally, the cry of a baby came from within one of the lodges. The horses' restless feet and soft whinnies could be heard as the boys gathered them into a single bunch to trot down to water in the river and then move on for grazing.

As I stood in the cool morning air, a breeze swept down from the mountains, pushing back small wisps of my long black hair. I looked around at the quiet camp just beginning to stir and thought of how my life would change as I moved forward to meet new responsibilities.

I was fifteen when I married the first time, Granddaughter. It was a traditional marriage, arranged by my brother and a paternal uncle. My mother and father had passed away, and my sisters were both married. I was welcome to live with either sister, but the males in my family, often away hunting or involved in war parties, were concerned about my future. My brother chose a kind and considerate young man from another band who was unrelated and seeking a wife. Abiding by the families' wishes, I became his wife. It was a reasonably happy marriage. My husband was seldom home, but he provided well for me and was excited to welcome two baby girls early in the marriage. Because of this man's kindness, I never questioned my feelings. I admired and respected him, but I was not in love with him.

However, when the news came of his death in a hunting accident, I mourned for him and wondered how I would care for my young family. One day Sharp Nose came to me to offer help. He had been a close friend of my husband's, and he quietly explained that he would always help my brothers keep meat and other supplies in my lodge.

The mourning period for my husband passed, and I became aware of this strikingly handsome warrior, Sharp Nose, whose generous heart was always tuned to his people. When he came to tell me my last remaining brother had been killed in battle, he gently held me in his arms and comforted me. He also told me how much he cared for me and that he would watch after my family.

As time passed, I realized how much I loved this man. He was kind and generous, and I was physically attracted to him. When he asked me to be his wife, my heart soared with love and happiness. I accepted his proposal. This was my second marriage, and no males were left in my family to negotiate the marriage, but there was a traditional exchange of gifts between the females of the families. A new lodge was erected for Sharp Nose and me. The female relatives called all the men into the new lodge for a feast. There was no ring or other symbol of marriage. When the two of us moved into the new lodge, it told the people we were a newly married couple.

My new marriage began happy and strong. I did not know how much this happiness and strength would help both of us endure the hardships the

Arapaho people would suffer over the next several years. I was happily un-aware of the events taking place outside my world. Those events would affect my life on the prairie, bring confusing changes, and lead to the loss of many friends and family members.

Grandmother, how excited you must have been, starting a new marriage during this time. I believe it was in the early 1850s and somewhere on the Great Plains that history books tell of a hunter and scout named Thomas Tibbles. He was writing the white man's history and said, "No more beautiful coun-try was ever seen." I have heard from the elders that it was in this great expanse of wonderful country that you made your home as you traveled with your husband and his band of Arapahos. Even today it is a land of great natural extremes, from the Badlands of the western Dakotas to Nebraska's endless sandhills swept by relentless winds. The Grandfather Winds are constantly busy. They bring dry blasts of air to parch the earth as they pass. They bring in cold fronts that roar down to surprise those who aren't prepared. The Grandfather Winds also bring the blessings of rain along with violent electrical storms and resounding thunder. Inches of rain can fall within minutes. Large hail can fall on the grasslands, battering the grass, trees, and birds that ignored the storm warnings.

Arapahos were in tune with Mother Nature, I know. My father told me how their keen sense of smell could detect a blizzard on the way and prepare the camp for icy winds and drifting snow. Rising early on a spring morning and turning to the southwestern mountains, Arapaho people could smell the first hint of the warming Chinooks that covered the grassland like a blanket, melting the snow and leaving little bursts of greening plants to emerge. Mother Nature was generous to the Indian people with her colors. She painted the prairies a glistening white in the winter, green with promise in the spring, and the soft yellow of curing grass in the summer and then produced the brilliant colors of turning leaves for the fall.

I was fortunate, Granddaughter, to have lived during a time when the air was pure, the rivers were clean, and food was abundantly provided by the four-leggeds that roamed the prairies, the foothills, and high into the mountains. The buffalo was the most important animal in our lives. No animal ever gave us as much as this denizen of the prairie. Subsistence for our people centered on the buffalo, physically and spiritually.

The Old Ones knew the buffalo was our best friend and that nearly everything we had came from him. The meat was tasty and healthy, and we used the skins for our lodges and clothing. From the buffalo we made clothing, carriers and litters, halters for the horses, saddle coverings, containers for water and cooking, and boats to navigate the rivers and lakes. We twisted the hairs into ropes. Buffalo sinews were used for bowstrings and for sewing clothing. Buffalo bones were shaped into spades, pickaxes, and food utensils. There were the songs of the Buffalo Dance, a ceremonial women's organization. Our people continued to honor the buffalo by using the skull in many religious ceremonies.

Yes, Grandmother, our history tells of one of the early Jesuit missionaries, Pierre Jean De Smet, who wrote in 1854: "The flesh of the bison is much esteemed and very nourishing; it is deemed the daily bread of all the Indian tribes on the Great Plains."

Granddaughter, the Creator and Mother Earth worked together to provide other animals for our people—for food, as companions, and as spirit animals for vision quests our young men undertook. The elk, moose, deer, and the fast-running pronghorn provided fresh meat and dried meat that lasted on the trail. We stored the meat and ate it when game was scarce during droughts or heavy winter storms. We often saw ground squirrels, prairie dogs, gophers, mice, rabbits, and snakes. It was a good omen when we spotted coyotes, wolves, badgers, beavers, wolverines, weasels, otters, and both black and brown bears. We treasured the birds for many reasons. They are our brothers, and we treat them with respect. We honor their place on Mother Earth—the hawks, the falcons, and especially the meadowlark (*jaw xu jaa nay he*), which speaks Arapaho.

The eagle has always been honored. He represents the essence of our people. He originates not only from Mother Earth and her elements but from the wonderful sky worlds above the earth, which are known as the spiritual worlds of the Creator.

Grandmother, I have been told that the eagle is respected, for he is the symbol of the greatness of the Arapaho people, and he continues to be the center of our ceremonies. We know him as the messenger to the spirit world. The eagle gives his wing bone to be used in the Sun Dancers' whistles. The Old Men use the feathered eagle wings in their medicine ways and in cedaring and praying for the good of the people. The eagle feathers are blessed. When one falls to the ground during a social gathering or ceremonial activity, there is a strict ceremony for retrieving the feather from the ground.

The eagle is revered as the denizen of the world above us, and he shows his authority through ferocity and purity. He travels skyward where the air is clear and is close to the Creator. Messages and prayers from the people are sent to the Creator through the eagle spirit. I have learned that not every man may hunt the eagle. The chosen hunter must fast for four days, abstaining from both food and water, and medicine is put on his hands before he is ready to catch the eagle. A pit is dug in the earth and covered with brush under which the hunter is hidden.

I know special respect has always been shown to the animals given to us by the Creator and Mother Earth because they are the substance of Arapaho life on the Great Plains.

Chapter Six

Granddaughter, you have listened well. Now let me share some things about the Arapaho that you should know.

In the early years, the Arapaho Tribe was too large to travel and hunt as a single group. There were too many people and horses to feed from a single hunting ground. For that reason the people divided into two main groups, the Northern and Southern Arapaho. Both traveled over the great divide between the waters of the Missouri and those of the Columbia. Then they would turn southward along the mountains. The Northern Arapaho, including Sharp Nose's band, camped at the head streams of the Missouri and the Yellowstone, in Montana and Wyoming. The Southern Arapaho preferred to camp on the headwaters of the Platte, the Arkansas, and the Canadian rivers, in Colorado and the adjoining areas.

From early times the Arapahos have been at war with the Shoshone, Ute, Pawnee, and Navajo, but we have been mostly friendly with other neighbors.

To understand our people, Granddaughter, you must learn about the five original groups of Arapaho. Some had unusual responsibilities. Each group spoke a slightly different language.

First, the Northern Arapaho consist of the *Ná'kasinĕ"na* (Sage Brush Men) and the *Ba'achinĕna* (Red Willow Men, Blood-Pudding Men, or Mother People). This group has always kept the *seicha,* or sacred pipe.

Second, the *Na'wunĕna* (Southern Arapaho), or *Nawathi'nĕha,* live in Oklahoma. They were placed there in 1867 and are called "southerners" by the Northern Arapaho.

Third, the *Aä'ninĕna* (White Clay People), or *Hitu'nĕna* (Begging Men) or Gros Ventre of the Prairie, later settled in the Montana area.

Fourth, the *Baä'sawunĕ'na* (Wood Lodge Men) were originally a distinct tribe and were at war with the Arapaho. Over the past 150 years, however, they have become part of the Northern Arapaho.

The fifth group, known as the *Ha'nahawnena* or *Aanu'hawa,* meaning unknown, lived with the Northern Arapaho. This group is now considered extinct, having blended completely into that tribe.

Remember, Granddaughter, that for most of the year the Northern Arapaho split up into three smaller bands. A band was a group of related families, and each had an important chief. There was the Forks of the River Band under Black Coal, who was head chief of the whole division. My husband, Chief Sharp Nose, was in charge of the Bad Pipes Band. The third band was known as the Greasy Faces and was led by Chief Spotted Horse.

Three other bands—the Long Legs or Antelopes, the Quick-to-Anger, and the Beavers—were also known to have existed at one time. These band families may have married into and become a part of other bands, for they no longer exist as separate groups.

Twice a year, in the fall and the spring, the entire tribe would come together to hunt buffalo. The biggest, most exciting event of the year was the Sun Dance, which took place in the summer. What a wonderful sight it was. I enjoyed watching each band move in and find its position in the camp. While people were still coming to the location, the chiefs would stake out the gateway entrance. Once the entrance to the circle was established, all the people knew where to place their tepees. It was a thrill for me to help the men and women place the tepees in a circle with the openings facing the morning sun.

West of the center of the circle, the men placed a large tepee that would house the Sacred Pipe. The Keeper of the Pipe occupied the tepee all during the meeting period. The Chiefs' Council met in that tepee. My husband and the other chiefs spent most of their time there. Between the sacred tepee and the gateway of the circle was the sweat lodge of the older men's ceremonial age societies, called *Nānāhāxwū*.

All of us looked forward to this annual summer meeting. It was the most sacred event in our lives. We believe all law and order for the tribe originated with the Sun Dance. It came about to help the people live a better life. Our Arapaho Sun Dance is much the same as that of other Plains Indians. Each ceremony is meaningful. I took great pride in being one of the women who cooked for the men when they performed the ceremonies connected with bringing the poles down from the mountains. The women could watch but did not participate as the men erected the center pole; built the dance lodge, a shelter of poles set in a circle around the center pole; and placed the altar and the Sacred Bundle containing the Flat Pipe in their proper places.

The early word for the Sun Dance was *hāsā'ā*, meaning "tanned hide or robe," perhaps because each dancer had a hide or a robe lying in front of him. It is also called *ha 'sāyāt*, which means "sacrifice." The dancers fast to prove their worthiness to have their prayers heard and answered by the Creator. The time of the Sun Dance was one of prayer renewal and the beginning of a new year.

Later in my life, I along with others were dismayed and fearful as we learned the U.S. Department of the Interior had prohibited the Sun Dance. The 1904 ruling called the dance an "Indian offense," and participation in the Sun Dance carried a jail sentence.

I was so happy to see the huge circle of camps with their tepees, each camp alive with family and friends moving about—the men going into the Council Tepee to smoke, visit, and discuss the tribes' affairs; women cooking over the outdoor fires; the savory smells of the food; the sounds of children running about, eager to renew old acquaintances and make new friends. Competitive games were a big part of the social gatherings, and children quickly set up their own races and games of skill.

When the Pipe Keeper and his attendants took down the sacred tepee, it was time to move camp. No other tepee was allowed to be taken down before it. When our bands were on the move, the Pipe Keeper traveled on foot, carrying the Sacred Bundle on his back no matter how long the trip. Carefully chosen guards attended him.

The buffalo-hide tepees were ingenious for our migratory life on the plains. They were conical, with a framework of long, slender, straight poles—preferably lodgepole pines when available. The men trimmed the poles of all inner and outer bark. Usually, a tepee required twenty to thirty poles. The women set the poles firmly in the ground, then brought them together about three to four feet from the top. Tepees averaged fourteen to eighteen feet in diameter, and a family of four to eight lived comfortably in this space. I joined the other women in covering our tepees and furnishing the insides. For the cover, we dressed untanned buffalo skins. Next we fitted and sewed them together in one continuous piece. We needed fifteen to twenty skins to make the cover, depending upon the size of both the tepee and the animal skins. If tanned skins were used, they were generally white, except where smoke-stained near the top.

A narrow space formed the doorway, which closed with a blanket suspended above the opening and spread out with two small sticks. The opening could also be a triangular flap. A pole would be inserted into a pocket at the end to prevent the flap from closing. The flap gave a family privacy. Visitors stood outside and called your name if they wished to visit. If you did not respond, they would quietly go away and come back another time.

When the tepee was closed with a small fire going, we could keep the space warm even in the coldest winter. In the summer, the bottom of the tepee was rolled up to allow a breeze to move through, keeping the tepee cool. The breeze also discouraged mosquitoes and other small insects from entering the living area.

The women could set up a tepee in about fifteen minutes. When there was an urgent reason to move—perhaps a war party threatening nearby—we could take the tepee down in about three minutes, pack the family belongings, and be ready to move out in twenty minutes. Our tepees were furnished only with necessities. Beds were the most important piece of furniture. Our beds were made of slender willow rods, peeled and straightened with our teeth. The willows were laid side by side and fastened by buckskin or rawhide strings through holes at the ends of the rods. The bed was then stretched upon a platform raised about a foot above the ground. One end of the mat was raised up hammock style, using a tripod and a buckskin hanger. The border of the bed was often decorated with buckskin fringe that was sometimes beaded, and the exposed rods were painted bright colors. The platform section, covered with buckskins and blankets, became a couch for use during the day. Pillows were made of softly tanned hides stuffed with buffalo hair. I preferred the down of milkweed because of its softness.

I was responsible for dressing the skins, a task performed exclusively by women. As a child I had learned the steps involved in this difficult task by fetching materials and running errands for my female relatives. First, we removed the flesh and fat from the hide. Then we soaked it. We then scraped off the hair, unless the hide was to be used for a robe or a rug. Next, we soaked the hide in liver or brain boiled in water, stretching it and then softening the hide by scraping and rubbing it. We might tan the hide over a fire smudge. Each of these steps was time-consuming, difficult work. My female friends and relatives worked together, assisting each other in the process. We sang our favorite songs and told stories to help pass the time.

The Arapahos moved with the buffalo herds except during the winter months. We tended to stay within our own territory, moving only a few miles at a time. Our men hunted mostly in our own area and chose sites that offered good water, wood, grazing for the animals, protection from the wind, and lookout spots for security. Prior to the white man's invasion, lookout scouts had only to determine whether strangers belonged to hunting or war parties.

A sudden increase in noise from the waking camp brought me back to reality and out of my daydreams about early Arapaho life. Putting more wood on the fire, I noticed that the water supply needed replenishing. As I picked up a receptacle and headed for the river, my thoughts turned to the traditional duties that were always a part of Arapaho life. As a married woman with family responsibilities, I knew the spring months would be busy. It was time for tepee repair, using new hides from the fall and winter hunting trips. The new hides would be "smoked" for leggings, moccasins, and other articles that demanded hard wear. Spring is a time of renewal. I enjoyed seeing the baby deer and other new births among the four-leggeds. Each day flocks of ducks and geese quacked among themselves as they headed north in their graceful V-shaped formation. Our bands would be moving from winter campgrounds to new foraging areas and preparing for buffalo hunts to replenish dwindling food supplies. Although individual family hunts were planned, the men of the tribe hunted daily for food supplies, and women gathered early roots and berries. Summer would bring the social gatherings and ceremonial events, for which preparations began early in the spring.

I rejoiced in knowing that it is the nature of Arapaho people to be friendly, with a great love of life. Children are taught early to be kind to one another and hospitable to newcomers. Strangers are made welcome, and visitors are promptly offered something to eat or drink. The people enjoy a united spirit, sharing the joy of eating and visiting together. The community plan was for each person to care for others, as they in return would care for him or her.

Forgive me, Grandmother, but may I tell you what I have learned about the camp's social life when you lived on the plains? The elders have told me that socializing among the Arapaho was based on four levels of community action.

First, the closeness of band kinship built a special relationship within the family and among families. Families shared their food with others. While they ate, they enjoyed talking about the events of the day and telling stories about old times and past adventures. I know the women shared many tasks, such as going to the forest or the river for wood and water. I imagine the women, accompanied by their daughters, felt safer when they stayed close together as they wandered far from camp to pick berries and search for roots. I'm sure cleaning and tanning were made much easier by the com-

Powder Face, an Arapaho chief, 1870. His crooked lance indicates membership in the Arapaho Spear Society and he was one of the warriors who was expected never to retreat in battle. Courtesy, National Anthropological Archives, Smithsonian Institution (neg. no. 180-a-1).

panionship of several women in the group. It must have been a wonderful time for the children. They would have felt both free and safe as they moved among the families in the camp. There was safety in numbers, and it was natural for the men to hunt together. The Chiefs' Council carefully chose the leader and members of a war party. Their brave deeds and actions were recognized and honored when they returned to camp.

A second level of Arapaho social life was based on community. When all the bands came together for the annual religious events and summer social gatherings, I know it was a time of great excitement. The elders say this was the time to exchange news and discuss buffalo hunts. Everyone gathered to watch the men perform the honor dances and hold victory celebrations. Individuality was not encouraged, but each person was made to feel a part of all activities. Any friction, jealousy, or divided loyalties were discouraged, as they might lead to problems among the families. Humbleness and speaking well about people were expected and showed respect for our tribe.

The third and fourth levels of social life arose from the interdependency of tribal communities. Our families' close relationships encouraged everyone to work together at the annual celebrations, planning the activities and providing food for the many social and ceremonial events.

Granddaughter, the Old Ones have given you a good description of our social life. This pattern was followed by other Plains tribes as well. Now let us rest a bit because I have much to tell you about our ceremonies and the societies that supported them.

Chapter Seven

Granddaughter, let me tell you about our tribal ceremonies. We called most of our ceremonies *Bayaawu,* or "All The Lodges," except for the rituals involving the Flat Pipe and the Sacred Wheel. There were three main tribal ceremonies. The first and most important was the Sun Dance. The second comprised the male societies' ceremonies, and third was the Buffalo Lodge. We looked forward to the Sun Dance as a time of prayer and renewal. It was time to put old problems away and look forward to the new year with expectations of good health and happiness.

We also had ceremonies associated with the male societies. Societies played a vital and well-known role in the life of the village and the tribe. Only five Plains tribes—the Hidatsa, Mandan, Gros Ventre, Blackfoot, and Arapaho—had societies to which boys and men were admitted based on their age. Through the societies our people transmitted the unwritten laws of the tribe. Nearly every male, from twelve-year-old boys to the oldest men of the tribe, belonged to one of the societies. Those who did not belong carried no respect and were not permitted to take part in the tribe's public affairs.

Granddaughter, I learned many things about the age societies as I watched my brothers take part in them. I began to understand at an early age how the men and youths were organized into eight age-graded societies. There were both military and religious aspects to this spiritual grouping. As the men grew older, their societies were mostly religious in nature.

The first six groups dressed symbolically in war regalia. Both of my brothers began serving in the first two youth groups. Neither group had dance or secret rituals.

When my brothers were about twelve, they were ready to become part of the Blackbirds, the first society. They told me they were to learn patience and obedience. I saw that they assisted and observed the older societies. By the time they were fifteen or sixteen, they were initiated into the Star Society.

As my brothers moved up through each level of the societies, their responsibilities increased, and the older men noted their efforts. Silence was encouraged, and respect was highly important. As my brothers left the Star Society, they were considered young men and moved on to the Tomahawks, the first of the men's societies. This was a special occasion, and I joined other female relatives in preparing a feast to be served after the initiation. As the men completed their initiation, the tremolos of the proud women echoed across the prairie.

Between ages twenty and thirty, men moved into the second society, the (Lance) Spear Society. I remember being happy about my brothers' successful achievements, but with wars so close at hand I also feared for their safety. The responsibilities became more intense as they became warriors. They also watched over us when we camped, when the band moved, and when a hunting party moved out. If a tribal member violated the laws of the camp, members of the Lance Society were sent to destroy his dogs and tepee. If the crime was severe, his ponies might be shot, leaving him helpless. This society had special duties regarding hunting parties. They saw that all the necessary religious ceremonies had been performed before the hunt's leader gave the order to proceed with the kill.

The Lance Society was also called the Drum Society. Thunder, believed to be a supernatural being, was the symbol of the Lance Society. The clothing the members wore was made in special ways to identify them. The female relatives tanned the skins and provided beadwork and other decorations.

The men designed and constructed their own ceremonial clothing. Each part had special meaning and symbolized the men's importance to the tribe. As appointed protectors, men in the Lance Society were expected to lay down their lives if necessary to provide safety for the people. Five officers, or leaders, were chosen for their bravery. All society members held special respect within the tribe. I felt very honored when both my brothers were chosen as officers.

My father and two uncles were among the thirty- to forty-five-year-old men who belonged to the Crazy Lodge. My father was still a member of this society when he died. The Crazy Lodge men had served their people well in their younger days and were now permitted to participate in less war activity. They had been required to pass through all the lower orders. They now watched over the ceremonies, making sure they were conducted properly. I watched my father and the other men in this group dance back and forth through a fire until it went out. The dance was an imitation of the fire moth, which the Arapaho called crazy because the moth would hover over a flame until it finally flew into it and died. There was never any evidence of the dancers being burned or scarred, and it was believed they were unharmed because of the Creator's power to heal while accepting their prayers. The materials they used were white clay, eagle feathers, and sweetgrass. The last Crazy Lodge met in October 1913.

Granddaughter, I remember hearing my mother talk about the next society, the Dog Lodge. Members were sometimes referred to as Beggars, and they serenaded the tribe during the nights of the Sun Dance. Women were invited to sing with them but were not allowed to become members of the society. I believe my mother sang with them when she was young, but I never took part. The outside world knew little about this society, as it belonged to the Sun Dance and was not discussed.

As a woman I knew very little about the sweat lodge, *Jenäjä'xibed* (which women were not to discuss), and *Nänähäxwü,* which were very sacred lodges. Permission to take part in these lodges was given only rarely. To become a member, great sacrifices had to be made. In the sweat lodge the participant fasted for three days, sitting perfectly still. Often, props were placed under the man's armpits to help him achieve the absence of motion. The Sweat Lodge Society met for the last time in 1874. The *Nānāhāxwū* was an even more sacred lodge whose members took three to four days to be initiated. This lodge met for the last time in 1878. It makes me sad to think that our people have lost these ceremonies, as they were known to be very helpful to our warriors.

I was a participant in the third division, the Buffalo Lodge, or *Bēnotāx'wu.* Any woman over eighteen, married or single, could belong. The enclosure for the Buffalo Lodge was similar to that for the Sun Dance Lodge, except the framework was covered with tepee covers instead of tree branches. During the ceremonial dancing we held whistles in our mouths, much like the Sun Dance whistles, and we rocked our heads back and forth from shoulder to shoulder, following the rhythm of the drum. Our four days of dancing occurred in five different places in the lodge, moving in a clockwise direction. The space inside the lodge was considered sacred, and onlookers could only watch from outside. There was a buffalo head in the lodge, and we wore headdresses made of buffalo heads with horns. The woman who sponsored, or vowed, to give the dance also wore a sacred buffalo robe. Both my mother and I were sponsors. My mother made the vow when one of my brothers was ill, and soon after the dance he recovered. I made a vow to sponsor a dance when one of my uncles suffered a serious injury in a buffalo hunt. He also recovered. This was a beautiful spiritual and inspirational dance for the women of the tribe. Sadly, it ended in 1895.

The societies played an essential role in the camp lives of our people. Each society had its own tepee, or ceremonial lodge, and medicine bundle. Each group's apparel was respected by all and was never copied by others. When a new member joined, he would choose his ceremonial clothing and the way it would be decorated. Members of each group had special flags and staffs that identified them as they took part in tribal activities. Each society had its own songs, descriptive of the nature of the group and of the ideal of a warlike spirit—so necessary to protect the people. Songs and dancing played an important part in the groups; they were expressions of the spirituality of their lives.

I needed to know about these societies, Granddaughter, because my husband, Sharp Nose, expected me to understand and respect their importance as I took my place at his side. He belonged to the most feared Warrior Society, called the Bad Pipe (Clan-Dog) Soldiers. Their war paint was red, meaning Arapaho; white, meaning long life; and black, meaning happiness.

When Sharp Nose turned twenty-seven he became a chief. He did not inherit his chieftainship but was chosen because of his bravery as a warrior. Although Sharp Nose was young when he accepted the honor, the people selected him for his dedication to the safety of our people and his ability as a warrior in dealing with the white men.

Granddaughter, I loved Chief Sharp Nose for the man I knew him to be, but I also respected him for his honorable achievements during his years of service as a warrior and a chief for our people.

The Arapahos had four chiefs, and the tribe considered one of the four to be the head, or principal, chief. The chiefs were chosen carefully, as they had to execute the will of the people while conserving our customs, traditions, and religion. The chiefs came to council only for important tribal matters. When the council met, it included all members of the sweat lodge and the *Nānāhāxwū,* which brought in all the old men of the tribe. Only the headmen of the other men's societies were permitted to attend.

As mentioned in Chapter Six, the Arapaho had four bands: the Greasy Faces; the Long Legs, or Antelopes; the Quick-to-Anger; and the Beavers. When the bands gathered for a common celebration, either social or religious, they formed their own circle within the camp circle. Being born within a band gave one permanent membership in that band, and it was the practice to marry someone from another band so there was little chance the marriage partners were related.

In the early years a chief might be chosen because he belonged to a certain band or followed in his father's footsteps; in my time he was chosen because he was a proven leader in dealing with the constant threats from the white man. When Sharp Nose became chief, he knew he would hold the position for life. If his conduct became questionable, he would lose the respect and obedience of the people and might be ignored, but he would retain his position.

Chief Sharp Nose, however, proved his worth to the people over the years, earning the respect not only of his own people but also of the military men who had initially been his most feared enemy. He gave evidence of bravery as a warrior and was effective in protecting his people. He proved himself trustworthy, both in battle and in peacetime, and his actions and decisions showed good sense and judgment. Although he was young when selected as a chief, Sharp Nose's courage during his years of service to his people showed the Arapahos' wisdom in choosing him to lead. I was proud to have my tepee set up in his camp and to know that every day I worked with and for him I was serving my people in the true traditional Arapaho way.

We were camping in the Central Plains area, in what is now Colorado, when we first heard the news of the white men needlessly slaughtering the buffalo. According to the white man's history, the last of the buffalo east of the Mississippi had been killed by 1832, but at the time I had no idea that the destruction would continue to move west and destroy the lifeline of the Arapaho people. As I listened quietly to the talk, it was hard to believe anyone would want to massacre buffalo in this manner.

There were rituals and ceremonies associated with hunting the buffalo. I saw the men shake their heads in disbelief. This honored animal was respected for the food and other articles it provided. I thought, Granddaughter, about the many times I had watched the buffalo hunt with great excitement. I knew we would take only what we needed for food. That night there would be celebration in the camp as our hungry families prepared the meat and feasted far into the night. The Creator had once again provided us with food. How could these newcomers to our world abuse this hunting privilege?

In another ten years the plains would resound with sadness over the deaths of millions of buffalo for no apparent reason, except that many thought if the buffalo were eliminated, the Indians would be more easily conquered. I would live through this infamous history of destruction, and my people would suffer from hunger and deprivation as a result of the slaughter.

But for now I put all worries aside and began to help prepare the camp for a move. Word had been sent that the Arapahos would go up north to visit relatives, the Gros Ventres. When we returned we would start moving south to be ready to take part in the treaty councils. My memories of the journey to Fort Laramie are clear. Thousands of white people were traveling across the plains on the Oregon Trail, and we heard the U.S. military had purchased Fort Laramie in Wyoming. The U.S. Indian commissioners held the first Treaty of Fort Laramie with representatives of the Sioux, Cheyenne, Arapaho, Crow, Arikara, Assiniboine, and Gros Ventre tribes. The tribes defined their territories and promised not to bother the wagon trains. Those who took part expected the government to comply with almost every treaty provision. They did not expect twenty-two years of war on the Great Plains.

I watched in amazement as tribal group after tribal group came in to take its place in the gathering. Never had I seen so many different tribes in one place, and it was a little fearful, as I knew many of those tribes had sent war parties into my homeland and warriors from my tribe had quickly responded. Now they all met in peace, but I felt uneasy and stayed close to my camp.

Sharp Nose had become a chief a year before the first Treaty of Fort Laramie, and he learned more and more about the white man's ways as he took part in the treaty meetings. He knew he carried a heavy responsibility in trying to decide what was best for our people as he prepared for future treaty councils.

Granddaughter, I married when I was young and accepted the duties of wife and mother at about the same time in life that you were starting your education among the white people. I understand that those were difficult years, and I would like to hear more about them.

Chapter Eight

Grandmother, let me tell you what it was like for me to go to the white man's high school. I encountered much prejudice, and at times I let it overshadow my potential for achieving an education.

Aunt Jean had attended the Thermopolis High School with no problems. She went directly to the university in Laramie, where she secured her teaching certificate. Her success made my reluctance to stay in school difficult for the family to understand. To my family's credit, they never expressed the idea that I was less intelligent than Jean or incapable of learning. They knew my problems revolved around my ancestry, but the family believed I should accept the cultural differences in a more positive manner. For a thirteen-year-old, dark-skinned Indian girl who had finally overcome the negative slurs hurled at her in grade school, the nonacceptance by many of my teenage peers was difficult to overcome.

Uncle Lester's solution to this dilemma was to send me to an Indian boarding school in Kansas. This seemed beneficial to my well-being because there would be other Indian students at the school. I was tired of being belittled because I happened to be Indian. When I asked about Indian teachers at the school, the answer was "No, there are only white teachers."

Nevertheless, the decision appealed to me. Knowing I owed my uncle a debt because of my unsatisfactory behavior during my last days of high school, I agreed to go.

Once that decision was made, I took the ranch dog, Bob, and hiked to the top of my favorite hill to look off in the four directions. I am convinced my Arapaho ancestors were showing me the way to make choices, even though I didn't fully comprehend it at the time. It was time to contemplate with the "powers that be" what my future might be out beyond the mountain ranges that enclosed the valley and shut out the rest of the world I wanted to see. Grandmother Anna, a Christian woman, had not yet thoroughly indoctrinated me into her religious patterns, but I recognized a higher power and, much to her consternation, referred to the Creator as the "powers that be."

As I looked over the valley, I knew I wanted to finish my education and find a way to make enough money to travel around the world and study cultures so very different from my own. Marriage and children would come in good time, but for now I wanted to be free to seek more understanding of the people of the world and how we all fit together on Mother Earth. How would the world treat my children and grandchildren, and would they be discriminated against just because they were Indian? I wanted to be proud of my Indian ancestry and have people accept me the way I was. Maybe at this school I would meet Indian kids like myself, and they could teach me how to be accepted.

I have never talked to anyone else about my experience at Haskell Institute, Grandmother Goes In Lodge, not even when other Indian people were telling of their good or bad times at the school. Why? I don't really know. It was such an empty time in my life—failed expectations of learning, seeing the bad effects of controlling people, the do-gooders deluding themselves in thinking they were doing good things when, in reality, they weren't. But it wasn't all bad. I met some wonderful Indian kids and made many good friends. Let me tell you how it was.

I had never been out of Wyoming, so the bus trip to Lawrence, Kansas, was exciting. Years later, young people going to school at Haskell would have a bus provided for them, and they would all ride together from a central point on the reservation. I did not have that support. I boarded a Greyhound bus in Thermopolis and traveled across the prairies to Lawrence. I had never ridden in such a big bus and had no idea about the stops and changes, so I watched everybody else and followed their actions. I sat close to the driver, as my family had suggested, and occasionally I would ask him about the cities or get directions about changing to another bus. It was frightening at times being on my own, especially at night when everything looked strange. But I was determined to make this an exciting adventure. I enjoyed the changing landscape and watched the endless parade of people in the towns as they went about their daily lives.

I was pretty scruffy-looking when I arrived three days later, but my identification was pinned to my clothes and luggage as requested by the school, and school personnel met me at the bus terminal. I was taken directly to the dormitory that was to be my home. I was not impressed by the long row of white cots, both in the main sleeping room and on the sleeping porches. My suitcase was turned over to the matron. My soiled clothing was checked in, and she issued me clean clothes every day. There was an initial body inspection by dormitory personnel to check for impetigo and pediculi (lice). I suffered through that indignation and began to think about how soon I could leave this place and return home. Twelve hours a day in the hay field seemed like a piece of cake compared with the personal degradation I was enduring.

The matrons were cold and impersonal, speaking in tones that carried the message that they were in charge and you were to do what they told you to do. Nothing more. The discipline at the boarding school was strictly military. A bell woke you up in the morning, and you had to fall into formation downstairs in the main hall. You answered to roll call. If you didn't answer, somebody was sent to find you. It quickly became apparent that it was not worth the effort to try to steal additional sleep. The duty detail one was assigned for laziness was true punishment.

I was used to getting up early at the ranch and had loved the early morning chore of rounding up the horses for the day. The fresh dewy smell of the grass and trees along the creek in the early dawn had been invigorating. I had seen birds fluffing their feathers and stirring about in the treetops. I had listened to them chirping to one another as they awakened to the rising sun. It had been a great way to start the day. But at this school there was no appreciation of a beautiful morning. At the sound of a bell you were expected to jump out of bed, comb your hair, brush your teeth, and put on whatever clothes were left at the foot of your bed. In fifteen minutes you were to be downstairs, wide awake and standing in line when the matron blew her whistle for roll call.

My dormitory was just for girls. We had our companies by grade (that is, all ninth graders were together, all tenth graders were together, and so on), and we drilled with the officers in charge. After breakfast we marched to our duty stations and worked until class time. I was assigned to the dining room. It was actually an easy job—setting tables, filling the condiment containers, and making sure the proper glasses or cups were in place. I had been doing these tasks at home since I was six. After a meal we cleared the tables and put on clean tablecloths for the next meal. When everything was done we headed off to class, still marching in groups. The worst part for me was the whistle blowing to remind us of what to do next—as if we couldn't remember from one day to the next what we were to do.

The classes were easy for me, but I remember little about what we actually studied. The dormitory time is what drove us crazy. We never had a free moment to ourselves. We even studied in groups. We always had our ears cocked toward the end of the hall so we could hear the first whisper of the matron's shoes as she tiptoed up the stairs to check on our studying. When it was time for lights-out we usually had so much pent-up energy that it was hard to lie still and go to sleep.

I met some wonderful kids at school. They came from all over the United States and represented many Indian tribes. I liked that part of school and quickly made friends. Many students were homesick and cried at night. They wanted to go home, but each morning they got up and struggled through another day. The older kids became indoctrinated by the system. They began to enjoy school and were granted more privileges. It was the younger ones who suffered. They were used to large, extended families and freedom to move among them.

As the first month passed, the unhappiest girls in our dormitory began to cling together to support one another. I was not homesick, but I didn't like the discipline and the matrons' behavior. I once saw a matron pat a little girl on the shoulder because she was crying, and then as she walked off she rubbed her hands on her apron as if to wash off having touched the girl. At first I felt sad for the girl, and then it made me mad. Why did this woman work among us if she felt we were untouchable?

Boredom and unhappiness become the devil's workshop. A group of us began to try to do forbidden things without getting caught. At night, after bed check, we put rolled-up blankets in our beds and went into the closet to play cards. Someone had swiped candles from the laundry building, and we would place a candle in a dish lifted from the dining room. By pushing all the clothes back in the closet, we had a nice little nook in which to play cards all night. It never entered our heads that one slip of the candle could have burned the whole building down and us with it. I think we were so unhappy and lonesome for our families that we were just living for the moment.

We had great success at this adventure, so next we decided to take midnight rides on the fire escape. The building was fairly old and had the round, enclosed aluminum fire escapes you could enter on each floor, then go around and around until you sailed out the bottom. The old gray U.S. Army blankets issued to us were great to wrap around us, and we would fly down the fire escape. This became one of our great weekend treats because fewer matrons were on duty then. However, one fall weekend, at the midnight hour, we were having a great time when the first girl sailed down, making no noise when she landed. She failed to dash out on the grass to encourage us on. We each took our turn in the now-eerie silence. I was the last to go. I was eager to hit the bottom and find out what was going on. As I zoomed out of the bottom, I spotted a pair of black oxfords. All the girls were grouped behind a very angry matron who grabbed me by the arm and asked if I was the last of these naughty, unruly, and ungrateful students who wanted only to make life miserable for those who did the most for them. I was in shock, but, quickly adjusting to the situation, I said, "I don't know. I heard some noise and came to see what was going on." The matron looked at the blanket wrapped around me and replied, "I just bet you did." That little adventure cost us many hours spent scrubbing big pots and polishing church pews.

In fairness to Haskell, it was a self-sufficient school, with the students' work helping it run smoothly. Many students adjusted to the military treatment and received an adequate education. It was not a happy place for me, and I became one of many who never returned for a second year. Several of us ran away. Each time we were forced to return, we became more unhappy. My uncle finally sent me a ticket to come home, and I gladly said goodbye to the place that had not fulfilled my expectations of freedom of learning and being accepted.

When the bus delivered me to my home after my boarding school experience, my family was happy to see me. However, Uncle Lester told me curtly, "All right, kid, it is apparent that you do not want to go to school. No, let's reword that—you will not go to school, so roll up your sleeves because there is a lot of work to be done on this ranch, and I am tired of promoting an education that seems to be going nowhere."

Having seen that brief smidgen of the outside world, I knew I would not be content to spend my time pitching hay, mending fence, branding calves, cooking for threshing crews, and doing all the other tasks that fill a rancher's busy days. I found a job in Thermopolis at the Carter Hotel, a resort near Hot Springs Park. After training for two days as a waitress, I was put in charge of the dining room. I had been serving food to people most of my life, so this was little different—except I was going to be paid real money. I had my own apartment at the hotel. I shook hands with Uncle Lester, said my farewells to the rest of the family, and went forth into the world to make my own way. My uncle's parting words were, "You want to go out and make your own living and see the world. Fine, but don't expect any money from me because you won't get any." We kept that agreement. I never asked for money, and he never gave me any.

The housekeeper at the hotel and I became friends, and we had many good times together. Her brother-in-law was only a few years older than me. She introduced us, and we started dating. Although boys were my second priority after my plan to see the world, I liked this young man. Unfortunately, he quickly became interested in marrying me, which didn't fit my agenda. I was still in my early teens and did not want to hurt his feelings, so I quietly left for a larger city—Casper, Wyoming.

Earlier, when I was eleven, I had spent time visiting my sister on the reservation. There I met a wonderful young Arapaho boy. He said he would come and see me when I was old enough to date seriously and to marry. That suited me fine, and I went home with a plan for the future.

There was a big hotel on the corner of Main Street and the highway through Thermopolis, called the Emery Hotel. It was the hangout for the cowboys and cowgirls during rodeos. When rodeo hands were traveling through the area, they always stopped to visit and catch up on the ranch and rodeo gossip. All of us local country kids liked to spend time in the lobby seeing who was dating whom and who was new in town. It was the place to be in the summer. Just before I left for Casper, the Arapaho boy came to Thermopolis and went into the Emery to find me. He hoped to take me back to his people. He asked around for me, and some boys I knew from Owl Creek told him, "Yeah, we know her, but she isn't interested in any old Indian guy, so beat it on back to the rez." He did, and he married an Arapaho girl a few years later. I never knew about this incident until he told me thirty years later when we were at the Sun Dance visiting and talking about old times. I often wonder how different our lives might have been if I had seen him when he came looking for me that day. We remained good friends until his death in 1994.

Chapter Nine

Granddaughter, it was spring. Chinook winds once again came sweeping over the prairie, melting snowbanks and revealing bright new blades of green grass. Tiny shimmering wildflowers greeted the sun each morning. The rivers were no longer covered with ice. Their muddy, swirling waters rushed along, giving evidence of runoff from the foothills. The rivers sounded eager to start the spring journey to an unknown waiting ocean.

Excitement was in the air. Everyone in camp—men, women, and children—felt the arrival of spring. We were ready to shake off the harshness of winter, breathe in the pungent scent of the new sagebrush leaves, and prepare to move across the plains.

It had been a good winter, with plenty of game in this valley along the Platte River, surrounded by mountains. The Grandfather Winds had blown cautiously during the swirling white blizzards, leaving the bluff tops clear for the animals to graze. Each fall the chief, on the recommendations of the Spear Men, chose the wintering camp. These men spent a lifetime learning the weather signs, and the location was carefully selected to protect their people. Extreme caution was used in choosing the site this year, as there had been rumblings that the white man was edging into the territory. Other

Arapaho tepees near Camp Supply, Indian Territory, 1870. The entrances to the tepees at the right are all oriented in the same direction, almost certainly east to greet the rising sun. Courtesy, National Anthropological Archives, Smithsonian Institution (neg. no. 45-d).

bands of Indians became nervous and were afraid to remain in one place too long. Winter spots were usually safe havens, but the Indians learned the white men never stopped for inclement weather. They pressed further and further west during all seasons.

But our Arapaho camp had been left alone, and now, with signs of spring in the air, it was time to find fresh grazing land. The horses were in good shape, and food supplies were ample, so the decision was made to move north. It was time to visit our relatives, the Gros Ventres. A flurry of activity greeted the news of the pending trip.

The children were caught up in the activity, helping with the packing instead of running off to play. I went about my tasks with a light heart, looking forward to the trip.

Granddaughter, the Arapahos and the Gros Ventres enjoyed a special relationship in our early days. They were one of the five distinct but closely allied groups, but we spoke different dialects. The Gros Ventres were detached from a larger tribe that included the Arapahos, but their traditions

Gros Ventres moving camp with a travois made by women and entirely wood and rawhide. The travois had side poles of stout lodgepole pines generally some four to five inches in diameter at the base. Courtesy, National Anthropological Archives, Smithsonian Institution (neg. no. 75.4268).

do not refer to a common origin with the Arapahos. They sometimes called themselves *Haa'ninin*.

The Gros Ventres were also sometimes called *Hitouunenno*, meaning "Greedy Man" or "Gluttons," possibly in reference to their characteristically large bellies. They form an independent tribal community but are closely akin to the Arapahos in language and customs. They are regarded as a subtribe of the Arapaho, and they later lived in an area now known as Montana.

Granddaughter, we were looking forward to this visit not only because our people had intermarried but also because of the common bonds between the two groups. Let me share some background on our relationship. The Gros Ventres had split off from the Arapaho when they migrated from the northeast in the 1800s. At that time they maintained a strong alliance with the Blackfeet. The Gros Ventres of the prairie practiced a series of age groupings that determined behavior between individuals and reflected particular tribal behaviors. The Blackfeet, as well as the Arapahos, also maintained this custom. All these groups had a definite system of age societies.

My uncle married a Gros Ventre woman, and she lived with our band for many years. She often discussed her people with us, and I believe at times she was homesick for her family. But she had a good life with my uncle, and she never complained. The Gros Ventres respected their women, allowing them to assist their husbands in the handling and care of medicine bundles. Women performed key roles in the Sun Dance. The women followed the tradition of having only two or three children during their childbearing years. Among the Gros Ventre, once a name was carried within the tribe, families usually retained it. It was believed that a person who had lived to a very old age had been shown distinction by the Creator, and families were encouraged to name their children after him or her.

I thought back to some of the stories I had heard about their hunting practices before they had horses and firearms. The Gros Ventres often hunted buffalo using a specially constructed, hidden area called a pound, or, as the Blackfeet called it, a *piskun*. The word translates as "deep-blood-kettle." The Gros Ventres had a well-known beast pound near the Saskatchewan River. It was a circle about a hundred yards in circumference. The ground was covered with trees laid one on top of the other at the foot of a hill about seven feet high. The entrance was on the hillside. The animals could easily go over the hill but could not return. This manner of hunting produced a good supply of meat for the tribe.

In the white man's year 1866, the Gros Ventres suffered their greatest defeat. They killed the Piegan chief, Many Horses, in a war. The members of his tribe retaliated, attacking a camp of Crow and Gros Ventres and killing over 300. The Piegans considered this the most decisive victory in their history, and the Gros Ventres recalled it as their most disastrous defeat.

I liked to see the Gros Ventre people dressed up. They wore showy, elaborate clothing, decorated with quillwork, beadwork, paint, and buckskin—very similar to that worn by the Northern Arapaho.

This spring's visit was to be a memorable one, the last of the carefree gatherings of our two tribes to visit and to trade. The threat of war was ever present, and treaties were being negotiated (and then ignored) across the plains. When Chief Sharp Nose sent his scouts ahead to announce the Arapahos' arrival, the Gros Ventres gave us a wonderful welcome. How proud I was to ride into this camp of friends and relatives as part of the chief's assembly. Our Arapaho band was given a place of honor as we camped among our friends and relatives from the north. The sun shone brightly on this circle of two tribes, coming together in peace and friendship. Even as he paid homage to his traditional way of life, each man in the Chiefs' Council knew these days were soon to change, and no one liked to think about it.

I watched my sister's two young boys with pride and respect as they approached the other boys in the camp and began visiting and planning games to test their skills. Following tradition, they left my sister's side at age six and began to receive instruction from the male sides of both families. I turned back to my daughter, Caroline (your grandmother), not yet a year old, who was wrapped snugly in her cradle board. She was sleeping soundly as I placed her close by so I could join the other women in preparing food for the feast that would follow the Chiefs' Council.

The Gros Ventres' camp lay in a valley close to the foothills of the Bitterroot Mountains. We had seen their scouts posted on the hilltops as we moved into the valley. The scouts, having already greeted our Arapaho scouts who went ahead of the troop, made themselves known as the tribe arrived.

Within minutes of our arrival, excitement spread through the camp. Women were laughing and sharing hugs. Children raced about showing off, as children do when company comes. New babies were brought out to be admired and fussed over. The horses, tired as they were, seemed to take on new life as the young men led them to the river for water and then drove them further out from camp to find fresh grass. Dogs raced around sharing the pleasures of the day.

The men gathered near the council tepee, and those privileged to do so entered to begin their visit. Others, according to their station in the age societies, had their duties to attend to. During rest periods the men would squat on their haunches and exchange stories of hunting and war party escapades.

The smell of cooking soon filled the air, as the women began to serve the feast to the men in the council tepee. When the Chiefs' Council members had been served in the lodge, the men from the different age societies gathered around the outside of the lodge and ate their meal. When the men inside the lodge were finished and the food utensils had been taken out, they would begin their meeting. It was customary to start the meeting with the traditional smoking of the pipe. Later, the other men would be invited in for general discussion and visiting.

Meanwhile, the children and women gathered to share food and talk. As soon as the boys were full, they rushed off to continue their games. The girls, laughing and sharing secrets with one another, helped us put everything away and ready the camp for the evening activities. It was a happy time. The drums were brought out, and the socializing went on far into the night.

Each day brought new activities, new friendships, and new opportunities for the children to have fun. The horses grazed further from camp, their sides filling out as the rest revitalized them. I enjoyed seeing the new colts romping around their mothers, whose shaggy winter coats were being replaced by new hair glistening in the sunshine. The warm, lazy afternoons passed swiftly, and it was soon time for us to move south.

One evening my husband, Chief Sharp Nose, gave the order to be ready to move out at daybreak. As the other women and I broke camp, I tried not to show my sadness, but our low spirits were obvious as we went about our work. I had a premonition I would never again enjoy a peaceful and joyous time with these same friends and relatives.

Both tribes were aware of uncertainty as we listened to the news brought into the camp. The white men were coming closer and closer to this territory, and things on the prairie would never be the same. The freedom of the prairie lifestyle was disappearing. How many of those boys lightheartedly playing their games of skill would lose their lives on the battlefield? How many of the girls laughing around the campfire would never live to see their firstborn? I braced myself and smiled as I prepared to leave. Arapahos never say goodbye; they only say "until later." And I was glad no goodbyes would be said as I hugged my friends before leaving. It was best to trust in the Creator and hope you would see everyone again next summer.

The weather was pleasant as our band moved southward. Soft, fresh breezes blew across the plains. Hunting parties were successful, and the camp moved at a leisurely pace. As we traveled further south, the evenings were no longer quiet and peaceful. I heard the women whispering about news of fighting among different tribes and of white settlers pushing westward. It never seemed to end. War parties often crossed our path, and they would visit with our warriors in camp. In the night I often heard the horses being gathered and the soft thud of hooves as the men rode out to join some conflict. Disquiet fell over the camp, as some men never returned and others rushed to meet in Chiefs' Council.

On the journey along the Platte River the fighting seemed far away at times. The women would gather berries and set up groups to work with the hides for new lodge coverings. New moccasins needed to be made and old ones mended. The work seemed to go faster when we met in groups where we could visit and share the duties.

One afternoon a small band of warriors rode into camp. The horses were matted with sweaty, grimy dust that lay heaviest on their manes and fetlocks as they headed down to the creek for water. The warriors slumped over their horses, showing the strain of long, hard hours on the trail.

Watching each rider to see if any was from our camp and would need food and fresh clothing, I noticed a woman riding with the group. She, too, showed evidence of hard battle. Her buckskin shirt was torn in several places, possibly by low-hanging branches along the paths, and her long black braids were dull with dust. Her face was drawn with fatigue, but her black eyes observed the camp sharply as she rode with the others. I had seen her before but had never asked about her, as that would seem rude if any of her relatives were near.

Since only my sisters were present when I returned to the group, my questions about the woman were readily answered. In our tribe, women's duties centered on home and children, whereas men were responsible for war and hunting. Occasionally, there were notable exceptions; some women chose to take part in buffalo hunts and to join the warriors in battle. In some tribes they were known as manly-hearted women. The Arapaho paid little attention to them. It was their personal decision, and as long as they did their share of duties for the common well-being of the tribe, no one commented on their choice.

Other tribes had stories of their manly-hearted women charging the enemy in battle and counting coup along with male warriors. Their hunting skills were exceptional, as their lighter weight gave the horses an extra advantage during hunting maneuvers. Their hunts brought food into the camps.

As the woman drifted out of sight, I wondered if she had children. The grandmother and aunties would care for the children, as was the custom when young women were busy with their duties. Or maybe she was single and called all the little ones in camp her children. This would be acceptable and respected.

The summer passed quickly as the band migrated down the Platte River and into the Central Plains. Often the camps were quiet for days at a time, but the warriors came and went continually. The uneasiness worked its way through the camp, as more and more talk focused on battles, loss of lives, and unrest among tribes as they sought a solution to the conflict with the white man.

The Chiefs' Council met often. My husband came in and out of the lodge at odd hours. I did not question him but provided him with food and fresh clothing each day. Our relationship was a traditional one. He had his responsibilities and I had mine. Often he would be gone for many days at a time, and his sleep was fitful the nights before he would rise and leave at dawn. The two of us had little time to talk. The few times we did lay awake at night and visit were treasured moments, as I never knew whether he would return. That was the way of battles.

It was late fall, and winter camp had not been decided. We seemed to go about our duties in a waiting pattern. At last, things began to happen.

After the Chiefs' Council we were ordered to prepare for several days of traveling. We would make dry camp along the way. This meant we needed to take water in containers, since time would not be wasted looking for a stream to camp by. We were going down to Big Sandy to pick up members of the tribe who had been traveling and camping with the Cheyenne. Chief Sharp Nose had voiced great concern about what might soon happen in that area, and he wanted to move his people north to a safer place for the deep winter.

Most Arapaho families left the Big Sandy Cheyenne camp to join back up with Chief Sharp Nose and our band. Some women who had married to Cheyennes had chosen to go the Cheyenne way and remained with them. Urgency was in the air, and our band quickly prepared to head north. Once again there were several days of hard travel, making dry camps at night so we could move steadily across the prairie.

Soon after our band of Arapahos had moved up north, the Sand Creek Massacre took place. It became one of the white man's history's most controversial Indian conflicts. On a cold November day in 1864, more than a hundred lodges of Cheyenne and Arapaho were settled in a bend of the dry Sand Creek. Colonel John M. Chivington and his troops took up positions around the Indian camp.

Cheyenne chief Black Kettle raised both a white flag of truce and a U.S. flag over his lodge. In spite of these signals of peace, Chivington attacked. The warriors fought back briefly, but the suddenness of the attack—unexpected after the recent truce negotiations at Camp Weld outside of Denver—prevented any organized defense against Chivington's forces. At the end of the battle more than 200 Cheyenne and Arapaho were dead—more than half were women and children.

There was great mourning in our Arapaho camp up north when a messenger brought the news of the Sand Creek Massacre, and the women's wailing could be heard across the prairie. My baby, Caroline, was a year old, and I held her close to my heart as I grieved for my people and the Cheyenne friends who were lost to me forever.

Chapter Ten

Grandmother, my heart is still saddened when I hear the stories of the Sand Creek Massacre.

You might think it strange that at sixteen I would decide to join the U.S. Marines. It was during the year I was working in the U.S. Army hospital near Casper. I thought it would be a good way to see the world, since I wasn't saving enough money to do it on my own. Of course, I wasn't old enough to enlist, but I managed to convince the recruiter that I could verify my age through reservation records. They let me enlist but then rejected me because I wore glasses and they were planning to send me to the South Pacific. I signed up for the U.S. Navy Civilian Corps instead, and they began processing my papers, again for the South Pacific. My grandmother Anna found out what I had done and warned me that if any government men came knocking on the door asking questions, she was not going to lie about my age. Luckily, the government didn't seek out my grandmother to verify my age.

About this time I was vacationing in Idaho and met a young, strikingly handsome, redheaded man who was dashing about the countryside on a magnificent motorcycle. He was a wonderful artist, and he painted a portrait of me seated on his bike. We fell madly in love. His family was Mormon and I was Indian, but in our youthful enthusiasm we were sure we could make a life together work, and we got engaged. We went to a big rodeo in which he was entered in the bronco-riding contest. Even though he was a good rider, he suffered a serious injury during the last ride and was hospitalized. The day before he was released from the hospital, my navy orders came, so I had to go to San Francisco where I would board a ship bound for the South Pacific.

My only experience with long-distance transportation was limited to cars, one motorcycle, and the bus. I almost panicked when my orders included a train ticket to San Francisco. It was scary being alone on the train, but I had asked for this, and there was no turning back. I decided I could handle whatever came to pass. The coach was okay, but the dining car was great. I had tickets to eat all my meals there. When it came time to go to bed, I hadn't a clue as to what to do. A kindly old train conductor took pity on me and explained about berths and how one prepared for the night. I had a hard time going to sleep; I was afraid I wouldn't wake up and that all the people would be up and dressed and would observe me crawling out of bed unprepared for the day. By the third day I was a pro at riding the train and was enjoying the countryside, even though I never knew exactly where I was. I didn't care. I was traveling.

When I arrived in San Francisco I was given quarters, and I worked on Mare Island until the ship sailed. I was never told anything about the future; I was just handed papers and told to follow orders. When someone delivered my sailing orders, I was apprehensive about going aboard a ship. My sailing experience didn't even include a canoe or a float, just homemade rafts on which to explore small lakes. My first view of the ocean was exciting, but there was so much power in that immense body of water that I was reluctant to sail on it. Plus I couldn't swim. But this was my chance to start seeing the world, so I grit my teeth and walked up the gangplank with everyone else. It did help that we sailed at midnight. I had met several people at work who were also heading for the South Pacific on the same ship, so I had some moral support.

The ship was an old Dutch freighter made over to carry civilian and military personnel. My first day at sea was wonderful. People around me were seasick, but perhaps because I was so excited about everything I never felt queasy. I was naturally slender, and at the ranch I ate as much as the heartiest cowboy. Onboard ship I went to the dining room for every meal even if no one was there but the crew and me.

Grandmother, one event stands out in my memory of this journey into the unknown that I had waited so long to experience. I was roaming around on deck one evening when I started talking to a young sailor from the ship's crew. He said, "Don't look at me while we are talking because we are not allowed to socialize with the passengers." So he worked close by and I stared out over the ocean as we talked. That night I hid in one of the lifeboats, and when he got off watch, he crept in and we talked until just before daylight. There was nothing inappropriate about our behavior. He missed his hometown of Brooklyn, New York, and we were amazed at the differences in the ways we had grown up. He couldn't imagine towns being separated by hundreds of miles of prairie. When I told him I was Indian I don't think he believed me because his first question was "Why are you dressed like everybody else?"

Two nights before we were scheduled to land in Hawaii, he said he had watch in the crow's nest at midnight. He gave me a pea jacket and a woolen cap and told me to put my hair up in the cap, wear dark trousers, and meet him by the lifeboat at midnight. I knew my uncle Lester would have asked, "Is this right, or are you going to be doing something wrong?" But the love of adventure won out, and at midnight I was ready. He said, "Follow me and don't talk." We walked to the base of the tower, and he said quietly, "One step at a time, and don't look down. And use both hands to hang on." We made it to the top. As we started around the top, we met another sailor who said, "Oh, you have company for a while tonight." My friend replied "Yeah," and we kept walking. The other sailor said, "Boy, I'm tired. It sure has been quiet, and it was hard to stay awake. Goodnight." I think we both started breathing again when he disappeared down the ladder. My friend said, "Okay, now you can look down, but hang on tight until you get used to the swaying."

It was incredible. I will never forget how the ocean looked that night, Grandmother Goes In Lodge. I felt as if I was next door to the Creator, as only He could have created such beauty. The moon was nearly full, and the ripples of the waves caught the moonlight with an explosion of tiny lights across the water. A soft breeze was blowing, causing the tower to sway gently. The low creaking of the ship as it met each wave was nearly lost in the swishing of the waves as they parted around the ship.

The young sailor tended to his duties, leaving me in the silence to watch the ocean—a constantly changing panorama. Later, as dawn broke, I said goodbye to my friend. He showed me how to back down the ladder without looking down. This had been such a fabulous experience that I had no fear of falling. I returned to my quarters and got ready for Hawaii.

The island of Oahu in the Territory of Hawaii, as it was called when I arrived, created many memories for me. The new job enabled me to live an independent lifestyle. For the first time in my life, nobody cared about my nationality or ethnicity. Hawaii was known as the world's melting pot, and many nationalities walked the streets and drove the roads. With my long black hair and brown skin, most people thought I was a *kanaki* (Hawaiian), and when I shopped in the local markets I paid local prices.

I worked for the U.S. Navy on Ford Island in Pearl Harbor. I lived on a mountainside, and it took four bus transfers, for a total of five buses, to get to the ferry to Ford Island. I didn't mind. The countryside was so beautiful, with flowers, trees, and shrubbery; and the lush green was certainly different from the Wyoming prairies I had just left. In the mornings I passed a small school as I walked to the first bus stop. Young children—white, black, brown, and every other color and nationality—were holding hands, hugging one another, and skipping around in the sheer delight of knowing one another and playing together. I thought, this is how the whole world should be. Adults should keep this unawareness of cultural difference and not sully it with the ugly discrimination and prejudice I had seen in my short lifetime.

Hawaii was a great place to relax and adapt to whatever came along. You could count on a temperature of 80° every day, plenty of sunshine, and an occasional shower to cool things off. From the minute I arrived I felt at home on the island, and the experience turned my life in another direction.

No hospital job was available when I reported to Ford Island, so my orders were changed, and I became an employee of the U.S. Navy Public Works Transportation Department. They asked me if I could drive a navy bus around Ford Island. I said yes, although I had never driven any motor vehicle in my life. The bus went around the island twenty-four hours a day providing free transportation to military personnel and civilian workers. It traveled at only fifteen miles an hour, so I thought I could learn on the job.

The current driver was to make a couple of rounds with me to show me the stops. She started the bus and shifted into gear, and we began our trip with me watching her every move. Then she told me to drive around a couple of times and she would monitor my stops. With much grinding of gears, we made the first few stops. As the bus emptied she asked me, "Honestly, now, have you really ever driven a bus?" I admitted I hadn't. She laughed and stayed onboard until I could shift the gears and make the stops without throwing people around. This was great fun, and I met a lot of interesting people. Then a transportation tech position opened, and I began an office job.

The people I worked with were great. My two best friends were a local white girl and a Chinese girl. They thought the fact that I was American Indian was pretty special, and we had great times together. There was lots of socializing in the evenings. Somebody was always having a party or a luau (a Hawaiian feast). There were United Service Organizations (military service clubs) downtown for the servicemen, and I joined a dance troupe at the Breakers and did two performances one night each week. I never drank alcohol, so it was not a problem for me to be around the socializing and just have fun.

Within a few months I met a Texas sailor who became my husband; we were married for twenty-three years. Even before I left San Francisco, I had started worrying about marrying the Idaho boy because our religions and cultures were so different. I remembered the problems my uncle had voiced about a white man marrying an Indian, so I quit writing to that young man and considered the engagement off. In later years I apologized to him for my inconsiderate way of handling the issue. We are good friends today.

Hawaii is a land of romance, and ever since my first romantic encounter I had spent a lot of time being in love with love. On the island of Oahu the beautiful moonlit nights, soft ukulele music, and enchanting aroma of tropical flowers all conspired to increase the affection the handsome Texan and I shared.

He gave me a ride to the ferry from the office one evening. As we drove onto the ferry he said, "You are one beautiful girl, and I think you are the one I want to marry." I laughed at him, as that was our first date. Yet two months later we were married. His sea time was up, and he could have returned to the United States, but he chose to remain with me in Hawaii. This was a wonderful period of my life. And it was about to get even better.

The day I learned I was pregnant was one of the happiest days of my life. I couldn't believe it was true. As I left the doctor's office I wanted to hop, skip, dance, and tell the world "I'm having a baby." A month later the doctor advised me to request a transfer back to the mainland because he thought I might have a difficult time during my pregnancy. My husband got orders for the States so he could accompany me. With regret, we said goodbye to those beautiful islands and headed home. As the ship left the harbor, we tossed leis over the side, as is the custom to ensure you will return. Over fifty years have passed, and neither of us has returned for a visit.

Back in the States we ate the foods we had been unable to find on the islands. Then we toured San Francisco. Since we had little money, we decided to save bus fare and hitchhike home to Wyoming. It was common during the years following World War II to see servicemen hitching rides along U.S. highways. Safety was not a problem. People were friendly, and crime had not yet reached the highways. We looked at the trip as yet another adventure, a time to see the countryside and meet new people. We laughed a lot on that trip. We were young and healthy with our whole lives ahead of us. We were excited about the baby-to-be, and life was good.

The people we met ran the gamut—the good, the bad, and the indifferent. The good tried to feed us all the time and shared their stories with us. The bad were caught up in drinking and smoking, and we cut our rides with them short. The indifferent just stared straight ahead and drove, with no interest in the world around them. But we weren't bothered by anything negative; we just snuggled together in whatever space the travelers gave us and watched the landscape change as we headed northeast toward the Continental Divide and home to Wyoming and my family.

Each new place was like another world. Leaving the sagebrush prairies of Wyoming and living in Hawaii had been like moving to a different world. After an enjoyable visit with my family, we caught a bus for Texas to visit my husband's family. Texas was yet another different world, but a good one. A little shock awaited us when we arrived. His parents had fifteen children, and all but three were at home. There was the traditional Texas barbecue, and people were everywhere. I loved it, and I learned to dearly love my mother-in-law. I called her Mama from our first meeting, and she treated me like a daughter. Throughout the good and difficult times in our marriage, she steadfastly remained the same loving and caring mother-in-law.

After our son, Jim, was born, we stayed in Texas and followed the rodeo circuit. This was an exciting time, and my husband was a good rider. But we finally decided it was time to settle down and let the baby sleep in a house instead of on a grandstand seat, although he didn't seem to mind. He was a happy baby and drew lots of attention from all the rodeo hands.

For several years we moved back and forth between Wyoming and Texas. We liked both places and loved being with our families. I was living in a white world, seemingly an uncomplicated one. My family would grow, and life would have its ups and downs, but even then my footsteps were starting to lead me back to my people. I just didn't know it yet, and I was not prepared for the changes that lay ahead.

Chapter Eleven

Granddaughter, the camp was unusually quiet that night. The nearly full moon reflected its brilliance off the silvery leaves of the sagebrush and rustling leaves of the cottonwoods. The lodges looked white in the moonlight, and the night sounds were muted. Even the rustling movements of the horses seemed quieter against the muffled sound of water in the creek.

Suddenly, I was wide awake. The soft sound of moccasins outside our lodge had been barely audible, but it brought me instantly to attention. I held my breath as I heard someone whispering my name.

Everyone was worried these days. So many war parties crisscrossing the soft, rolling hills brought strangeness to the once-familiar land. Where was the enemy today, and how could we know who the enemy was?

I recognized the caller's voice, and I went to the lodge flap, careful not to disturb my husband who could rarely stretch out in familiar surroundings and get a full night's sleep. He had returned late, exhausted from long days on the trail with one of his war parties. He had allowed himself to relax in a deep sleep because he knew I would awaken him at the first sounds of danger.

Softly, my friend explained that a friend's daughter was ready to deliver a baby, and her mother was requesting my help. I quickly slipped on a dress and reached for my parfleche, which contained the materials I might need. I glanced at my sleeping husband and prayed for his safety if he had to leave on his next journey before I returned.

As I stepped out of the lodge, I glanced at the sky and became aware of the beautiful moonlit night. Yes, this was a good time for a birth. A new baby to be welcomed into the tribe was a special blessing from the Creator, and I was happy to be a part of it.

No dogs stirred, and there were no other animal sounds as the two of us slipped between the lodges until we reached our destination. The lodge we were about to enter had a soft glow from the small fire inside, and the dark outlines of people moving about were clearly defined. Suddenly, I was aware of a man standing off to the side of the lodge, and I felt sure it was the husband of the woman I was to help. I could feel tension and restlessness from his presence. I knew he was worried. Perhaps his wife had been in labor too long, or maybe it was just the uncertainty of a first-time father. I smiled to myself as I remembered my husband's concern when I was in labor with each of our two babies.

As my friend and I entered the lodge, a quick glance about assured me that all was in order. Because of the possibility of having to move quickly in case of enemy attack, no special lodge had been erected for this birth. The baby would be born in the home lodge. The woman's mother and father were present. Her father sat near the back of the lodge, and her mother was helping an elderly woman, who was moving about in preparation. The older woman whispered that the Medicine Man had already given the woman a potion, *ponco,* made from a peppermint plant. I had been present earlier in her pregnancy when a young skunk had been dropped between the front of her body and her dress, a traditional assurance of an easy birth since skunks give birth easily.

I glanced around again as I moved toward the young woman. The medicine bags had been removed for a birth. That was good. Otherwise, they might become tainted and have to be removed within a day of the birth and cedared with bits of beaver testes on hot coals. The woman looked up at me and smiled, showing her appreciation for my presence.

The Medicine Man who had prepared her drink sat beside the woman's father. Directly to one side of them was the horizontal rod resting in the crotches of two upright poles the woman would hold on to as she knelt in position to deliver the baby. The rod was placed at exactly the right height to give her maximum pulling power while she knelt. Under her knees were soft hides stuffed with dried prairie grass and covered with an old blanket.

The woman covered her mouth to suppress a groan as her body stiffened with pain. In slow motion, much like a rehearsed dance, the players shifted into place. The woman knelt on the padding, reached above her head, and grasped the bar. As she did so, her mother pushed an eagle feather down her throat, making her cough and gag. The gagging caused her to push down, and her mother spoke softly, encouraging her to continue pushing with the pain. The older woman, a recognized midwife within the tribe, sat directly in front of the woman and prepared herself to receive the baby. The mother motioned me to take my place behind the birthing woman, place my knees tight against her buttocks, and clasp her stomach with both arms. The mother then stepped back and, sitting cross-legged to one side, prepared to wait. It would not be long.

Through the top of the lodge I could see the sky lightening. A soft breeze carried the smell of dew-laden grass and trees across the camp as the land prepared for a new day. The horses under the trees along the creek bank began to shift and stir. They were not ready to leave their warm spot, but hunger would soon bring them to their feet, and they would drift out to graze. In another hour the camp would awaken. The dogs would bring their noses out from under their tails, stretch, and begin to search for food.

Inside the lodge the woman's pains came closer together, and I knew the baby was ready to be welcomed into the world. The birthing ritual continued as the movements of the people engaged in the birthing merged and mingled. Each of us knew our role, and soon the newborn's lusty wails wafted out of the lodge and drifted across the camp, fading as the sounds moved across the sagebrush.

The older woman had promptly caught the baby and forced the fluid of the navel cord away from him. She tied the cord with sinew and cut it, using the length of her hands to measure the correct distance. The end of the cord was folded down against the baby, and buffalo manure, finely ground into powder, was packed around it. A clean cloth was wrapped around the baby's middle to secure it. The cord would drop off in about three days. The cord would be saved and placed in an amulet, as was our custom.

The Medicine Man prepared a cedaring of beaver testes over hot coals for the new mother. She was young and strong, and even though she had just given birth, she was able to stand over the fumes. She inhaled the fumes as the Medicine Man used an eagle wing to waft the fumes over her to purify her body in the traditional manner. He then left the lodge to inform the father that he had a new son. The father remained outside the lodge until the women finished their duties.

I quickly wrapped everything pertaining to the birth, including the afterbirth, into the old blanket the mother had been kneeling on. It would be taken out and placed high in the crotch of a tree, where it would remain unmolested until absorbed naturally by Mother Earth.

A warm feeling came over me as I sat close to the new mother watching the older woman give the baby his first bath, which consisted of splashing handfuls of cool water on his back. His lusty cries foretold the healthy future of a strong baby. She then handed him to the woman's mother, who rubbed his entire body with an ointment made of red earth mixed with softened buffalo tallow.

The baby was tightly wrapped in a clean blanket and given to the mother, who lay resting on her bed. I rubbed my hand over the baby's generous crop of black hair, which was standing up in glistening disarray. What a beautiful baby. I silently gave thanks to the Creator for the baby's good health and prayed for him to have a long life filled with happiness.

All the women stepped out of the lodge to return to their own campfires to begin breakfast. The sun was giving promise of a new day with a brilliant red glow just below the horizon. I had taken a moment to enjoy the beauty of the morning when a shout rang out, and I heard the muffled hoofbeats of horses running at full speed toward the camp. A strange foreboding filled me, as the horses never slowed but rushed directly to the Chiefs'

Council lodge. It was a scouting party returning. From their haste and excitement as they dismounted, it was evident that more bad news about the war was forthcoming.

Racing to our lodge, I saw my husband and several other men making their way to the council lodge. It was too late to make breakfast, but it would be wise to prepare dry food for a journey because the camp might have to move at any time.

Twenty-four hours later the camp did move. Time was taken to carefully plan the trip to avoid war parties and the ever-present raiders who seemed to lie in wait to steal horses from small, unprotected bands of Indians. Sharp Nose and his band headed south for the country (now called Nebraska) down the Platte River and across the rolling hills.

As the summer passed, more and more changes took place, and the tribes were forced to keep traveling across the prairie. Gone were the leisurely days of hunting and fishing, combing the shores of creeks and rivers seeking the bushes with the heaviest harvest of berries, and moving only when new herds of game were sought. The women were always on alert, with little time to prepare the hides for tanning; new clothing was made hurriedly. The men were constantly on the move, needing new moccasins more than ever before. Even the children, usually obedient and eager to play, seemed caught up in the whirl of camp preparation and no longer wandered far during playtime. A constant sense of danger loomed over us no matter where we moved. The sagebrush prairies and green rolling foothills were no longer the friendly and familiar places that used to welcome us as we chose a campsite.

At night, listening to the camp settling down, I could no longer slip into the secure, dreamless sleep I usually enjoyed. Instead I lay awake, listening for the sound of pounding hoofbeats and the warning words of the camp crier as he gave orders to prepare the camp to move out.

Even on the nights when no war parties came, I often lay awake until the morning light, wondering where my two older daughters were with their husbands in far-off camps unable to plan visits or send word of their welfare. It was comforting when my daughter Caroline and her friends and sisters (cousins) chose my lodge to sleep in. The small bodies lying close together and the rhythm of their soft, even breathing reminded me of earlier times when the girls, giggling in high anticipation, would have lengthy discussions about what lodge they would choose for their nighttime storytelling. With each girl's family and extended families, there were many safe and secure lodges in which they could sleep.

One evening, when my husband had returned after having been gone for several days, he called me into the lodge and asked to speak with me about an important matter. His manner was serious, but he was kind and respectful as he asked me to be seated.

Fearful that I had done something to displease him, I kept my head lowered as he spoke. We had always shared a great deal of love and happiness, even as our time together became more chaotic. His first duty was always to his people, looking out for their safety and welfare with little thought for himself.

I sat cross-legged close to the fire as he spoke. He sat down close to me and gently placed his arm across my shoulders. Inwardly, I was numb with fear as I sat quietly waiting for his words. He spoke softly as he thanked me for all the years we had shared and complimented me on my work with other women in the camp. The brother of a woman who had recently lost her husband in a battle on the Platte River had asked him to take her into his camp as a wife. She had children, and it would be hard for others to care for them.

Granddaughter, it is difficult to tell you my real feelings at this time. This was a traditional occurrence. My husband was asking me to accept another woman to share my married life. This did not make my position in his lodge any less important. In fact, the help from her would be welcome as I struggled to keep the camp in order during the frequent moves. Her children would become brothers and sisters to Caroline, which would be good.

I knew it was common for a chief with a large band to have more than one wife to accomplish all the work necessary to support his duties in caring for the band. But this was my husband and my lodge, and I must confess to experiencing a twinge of jealousy at having to share the man with whom I had such a close and intimate relationship. But jealousy is not the Arapaho

Wind River Reservation, Wyoming; from left to right, Winnieshead Sharp Nose, Jerome Old Man, and wife, Edna, Northern Arapaho, 1936. Courtesy, National Anthropological Archives, Smithsonian Institution (neg. no. 2004-14916).

way. Arapahos always consider what is best for all concerned. I would have to open my heart to this woman and make her welcome in the lodge as my husband requested. As I nodded in agreement to his proposal, he thanked me, gathered me in his arms, and held me close for a moment. Then he quietly left the lodge, and I began another new period of adjusting to my changing world.

Sometime later the woman's sister also lost her husband on the battlefield, and she joined the family as a third wife, bringing her children. So much was going on in the tribe's struggle for survival that families became closer and supported one another, with little thought for personal needs and wishes. It was not a time for individual concerns but rather was a time to focus on the overall welfare of the tribe. When I silently accepted my husband's request to take a second wife in the traditional Arapaho manner, I could not have known that long after my life ended, these two women would remain at his side for more than thirty years until his death in 1903.

There came a time when the Arapahos were living as fragmented bands, slowly marking time as we camped around the different forts—Fort Laramie, Fort Casper, Fort Smith, and Fort Robinson. The number of white men kept increasing. New discoveries of gold brought even more of them to the West. We knew nothing of this glittering rock except that it was valuable to the white man, and the white man's greed for our land increased. There was talk of moving the Northern Arapaho to Oklahoma Territory. My husband, Chief Sharp Nose, refused to go and headed north with his band.

It was a hot July afternoon in the Nowood country up north when the warriors of our camp responded to the war cries of the Shoshones. They fled to the top of a butte and prepared to do battle with both the Shoshones and the military. The women and children remained in camp while the battle raged. Later, I listened to accounts of the action and learned that on July 4, 1874, the white military leader, Captain Alfred Bates, accompanied by Chief Washakie, had been soundly beaten and forced to retreat. The Shoshones ran off with over 200 Arapaho horses, and our tribe lost 50 warriors. The battle remained clear in my memory because the action took place so close to the main camp.

The Cheyenne and Sioux joined our camps, and we moved north following well-known trails into Kaycee country. Others would move down to Fort Casper and Fort Laramie and spend the next winter in that area. The following year the tribes parted, creating a separation of the Arapaho Tribe that affected the tribe traditionally, culturally, and politically for many years to come.

For now, it was good to be on the move. Spring was in the air, but the Indian tribes did not have the gladness of heart that usually welcomed warmer weather. This would be another year of uncertainty, distrust, and hopelessness as we saw the white people taking over our lands. How would it end, and where would we go?

We camped close to the river. Things were expected to be quiet for a few days, and as I joined the other women to hunt for special plants and roots, I was called back to wait for the sweat lodge to be put up. I would need to help prepare the food later, but now I watched the rituals surrounding the construction of the sweat lodge.

The first thunder of spring had been heard. Willows had been gathered and placed in a lodge until it was time to build the sweat lodge. They were brought out, selected, and counted. Four women were called to come forth. Holding a stick, they put some of the willows for the framework in place. The willows were planted securely at one end and bent to form a dome-shaped enclosure that faced east. One woman went around the framework before it was covered with blankets and, as a blessing, passed her hands down each of the poles toward the ground.

When the sweat lodge was covered, a small pit was dug in the middle, and an altar was placed in the front. A buffalo skull with sweetgrass or sagebrush in the eye sockets and nostrils was placed on the altar along with other medicine bundles. A large fire had been built at the end of a path a few yards away. Many round river rocks had been laid in the fire in a special ceremony. The rocks were heated to a rosy glow.

The ceremony was ready to begin. Four men entered the sweat lodge along with a Sun Dance Elder. They were followed by a Medicine Man carrying a buffalo tail mounted on a short stick. A red thong wrapped around

Sweat lodge framework, Northern Arapaho. Courtesy, National Anthropological Archives, Smithsonian Institution (neg. no. 2004-14917).

the stick held several long, shiny magpie feathers. This would be used to switch, or whip, parts of the body receiving the medicine. When the men came out of the sweat lodge, their brown bodies glistened with sweat, and they went directly to the river and jumped into the cold water.

I knew another four men would soon enter the lodge and that this might go on for hours. At the end of the sweat, food would be prepared for everyone. At a nod from one of the other women seated around the sweat lodge, I arose and joined the others as they left the area.

As summer ended, our band again moved south. I heard talk that the band would be wintering in a place called Fort Robinson (Nebraska). My husband now knew the white man would never leave and that the safety and future of his tribe would depend on its ability to live in peace with the white man. I watched his face become more lined with worry each day and saw his tall frame slump with fatigue as he struggled to make good wartime decisions for his people.

I did not want to live near the white man. I was uneasy each time the band camped near military forts. I longed for the old days when the band could camp where it wished, the buffalo were plentiful, and the laughter of the people rang across the prairie. I longed to see acres of tepees shining in the sun when all the people gathered in the summertime; to hear the laughter of the children as they raced through the camp; to watch the Old Ones gather in the shade to tell stories and brag of the things they had done in their youth; to see the men clustered in groups telling stories about their relatives, followed by laughter as each one tried to outdo the other; to see the young girls staying close to their female relatives but casting furtive glances at the sleek, tanned bodies of the young men as they dove into the river after the heat of the competitive games. This was the life I longed for, and I suffered with the changes taking place. Perhaps the Creator heard my thoughts and made other plans for me. I would not see another spring.

When this Indian summer came to an end, Grandfather Winds turned chilly, and the band headed south to Nebraska. The land was familiar at first, but as the traveling routes changed, areas began to lose their familiarity, and it seemed an unknown land. There were no calls for a buffalo hunt; the big brown creatures so much a part of the Indian way of life had virtually disappeared. The buffalo was greatly missed, as that left only the antelope, deer, and elk to make up most of our dried meat on the trail.

It was somewhere in the Nebraska hill country that I fell ill. I had always been healthy, so when I caught a cold that wouldn't go away, I sought out our Medicine Man. He assured me that colds had to run their natural course and that in time I would feel better. Time passed, and I did not improve. My husband called in the Medicine Man again, and a long day of doctoring took place. My fever was high, and my husband lingered near the lodge, making sure I had water and anything else I needed. The other wives kept the children quiet and left me to rest. I knew the band should be moving on, but no lodges were packed. There was an air of quiet, hushed waiting about the camp. I was also waiting for recovery, but it was not to be. Death was near.

Four days later, at midnight, the tone of the Medicine Man's chant changed, and I knew he was bowing to the Creator and giving up. Although

I heard him lift the flap and leave the lodge, I seemed to be waking from a dream. Slowly recalling the dream, I remembered seeing each of my children happy to see me. Tribal Old Ones who had passed on long ago came into my dream to visit, shaking my hand in the soft Arapaho way and greeting me as if I had seen them only yesterday. My father and mother, as young as they had been when I was small, reminded me of the happy days at home. It was a true gathering of friends and relatives who no longer lived on this earth and came to say hello in my dream. I opened my eyes and glanced around.

My husband came to my side. I told him of my dream and smiled at the happiness I had felt. He held my fever-ridden body close, and I thanked him for all the wonderful years we had spent together. "I am sorry," I said. "I think I must leave you now." He held me tighter as if to keep me from leaving. The pain was gone from my body, and I sensed a light all around the lodge. In the distance there was drumming, and the songs were happy ones. I sighed as I relaxed my hold on my husband's earthly body. It was time, and I was ready. I closed my eyes and drifted into my final sleep.

Chapter Twelve

In the early years of my marriage, Grandmother, the frequent moves between Texas and Wyoming became a way of life. My husband and I not only loved our own families, but we had mutual respect and love for each other's families. The nomadic pattern we established allowed us to keep in touch with both of them.

Although I had no female Arapaho relatives to tell me early in life that having a baby was a blessing from the Creator, the children I bore became the greatest blessings of my life. They were like little miracles, each in its own way. Our first baby son, Jim, was given a great Texas welcome. Because of the difficult birth, we thought he might be our only child. When I was small I used to tell Grandmother Anna that I wanted a dozen babies. I was less enthusiastic following the reality of the first birth, but we did plan to have more children.

We were back living in Wyoming when we decided to investigate the possibility of having another child. The doctor I chose, Dr. Stack, practiced in Thermopolis. I had worked for him in the hospital when Jim was a baby. If no other babies were in the nursery, he allowed Jim to stay while I worked my twelve-hour shift. Dr. Stack was also a family friend, and I trusted him.

He listened carefully to my story, and later, when we met in his office, he assured me that if I became pregnant, he would deliver my baby. I said, "I'll be back tomorrow for my prenatal exam." He laughed, but nine months and two days later he delivered our second beautiful baby boy.

This wonderful and impatient baby arrived during a major flood. It was February, and the temperature had been −20°. The river was iced over from bank to bank, and several feet of snow blanketed the region. Then came the Chinook winds sweeping down from the mountains in their usual springtime manner, sending a steady flow of warm air over the valley. The snow began to melt, and water ran freely into the river, causing the ice to crumble. Great cakes of ice started their journey downriver. Occasionally, the blocks would cling to one another and pile up in high peaks, blocking the river and causing flooding.

When I was about to give birth, the ice had piled up against the bridge across the Big Horn River, and the water was rising to flood stage. My husband rushed home and got some of his crew to move our belongings to higher ground, and we left for Thermopolis in a flurry of ice and melting snow. Dark had settled in, and about six miles from our destination we saw the highway patrol's lights flashing. An officer waved us to a stop. He informed us that we would have to turn around, that the water was flooding under the bridge ahead and it was not safe to cross. By this time the baby was indicating that he would not wait for anything, flood or no flood. My husband explained the situation, and the officer quickly said, "All right, I see this can't wait. I will ease my car over the bridge, and if it holds, follow me and keep moving." We made it. Dr. Stack kept his word, and in a few days we returned home with our new baby boy, named Dennis after the doctor who continued to be our friend.

When my boys were small I saw very little of my Arapaho family. My father saw the boys occasionally, but our primary focus was on earning a living—which we could not do on the reservation.

We were living in Thermopolis. The boys were four and two when I was introduced to alcoholism at its lowest level, "the wino stage." Until then, my experience with drinking had been limited to seeing people come to town on Saturdays to shop and have a few beers with friends. Growing up and attending country dances in the valley, it was understood that the men went outside to share a drink or two, but when they became too bois-terous or unruly they were told to either behave or sober up. There was a lot of laughter and good-natured kidding about being intoxicated, but it never seemed to be a serious problem. During my dating years, since I didn't drink, my experience with uncontrolled drinking was limited.

One day I came face-to-face with a major problem within the Ameri-can Indian community, one that has grown increasingly worse over the years. It led me to work in the area of alcohol and drug prevention for many years.

My husband was working on the Boysen Dam project, and our lives were blessed with good friends, good jobs, and healthy children. Life was good. One fateful day there was a knock at the door, and when I opened it a young Indian man was standing there. He looked at me, smiling, and said, "Hi. Are you Virginia? I am your brother Bill, and I need help."

I had seen my brother briefly only once when I was a child. The picture of Bill my father had given me showed a happy twelve-year-old with a big smile. The man standing on my doorstep bore no resemblance to the boy in that picture. I invited him in, and we talked. He was very ill and never let go of the brown sack that held the stuff he lived on—wine, the cheapest he could find because he was also penniless.

Bill had joined the service, and when he was injured overseas he had been sent to New Mexico to recover. There he also learned that he had tuberculosis. He was put in a sanitarium for a short time and then sent home to the reservation. He told me he knew he was dying, but he couldn't quit drinking and he asked if I would help him. I did my best. I took him to Fitzsimons Veterans' Hospital in Denver, and he began to recover. We were excited to see how well he was doing, and we visited him whenever we could.

We had some good visits, but this story does not have a happy ending. Bill made rapid progress in the hospital; the tuberculosis was arrested, and he became well enough to be given a pass to town. He was enjoying his sobriety and wanted to share his progress with his less fortunate friends who hung out in downtown Denver. Unfortunately, on his way home one night—completely sober—he was mugged, robbed, and severely beaten. Back in the hospital, he again began the slow road to recovery, this time from a broken jaw and other severe injuries.

Meanwhile, my husband, sons, and I had moved back to Texas. One day I received a call from my sister telling me my brother was dying and had asked to see me. Apparently, the family had gone to visit him, and since he was homesick they agreed to take him home. He had returned to drinking with his buddies and was now dying. We left immediately for Wyoming and drove straight through, but we were too late. My sister told me that when Bill heard that we were arriving that day, he asked for a mirror and a comb to fix his hair. He told her he wanted to look nice for his sister. He handed the items back to her and thanked her. Then he lay back against the pillows, smiled, closed his eyes, and quietly passed away.

I arrived a short time later, and as I looked at his face, relaxed and free from the pain and suffering, the slight trace of a smile still apparent, I finally saw the resemblance to the laughing twelve-year-old in the picture. His life was over at age thirty-two. I was inconsolable. Today, each time I succeed in helping someone stay on the Red Road to sobriety, I think of Bill and dedicate my work in this field to the brother and friend I lost too early.

It was during those years that Wyoming became caught up in the big oil boom that swept the country and affected most western states. Rigs were constantly moving in and out. Jobs were plentiful for those who could endure the rough, hard work. The high wages, though, drew many people into the work. We soon joined that group and began traveling across many of the western states where the jobs were located. My husband was young, healthy, and a hard worker. He didn't mind the trips to the drilling sites, often sixty miles or more on almost nonexistent dirt roads. In the winter the weather and the roads were so impossible that the crews often had to work double shifts because the crew coming on couldn't make it to the site. My husband got along well with people, and he liked the work. He quickly advanced from deckhand to derrick hand to motor man to driller and then to tool pusher. Each position had its own dangers because the men worked on deep wells and moved a lot of steel pipe.

The wives and children would often pack a lunch and visit the rigs in the summertime. Each state had its own particular beauty, and we took advantage of the opportunity to see that beauty.

The only time I feared for my husband's safety was when he was a derrick man. We would watch him walking around a narrow platform high up in the top of the rig. He would stack the stand of pipe in neat, compact rows as it came up out of the ground.

I can still feel the warmth of the Montana sun on my back as I held my little boys' hands and looked up to watch my husband work. I can hear the hum and groan of the motors as the men brought the pipe up, the crashing, clanging ring of steel on steel of the pipe. He stacked the pipes in rows that enabled him to reverse the motions as each pipe went back into the ground. I recall the slap of the chain as it wrapped around the pipe and the yells and laughter of the men as they worked. There was camaraderie among these men who faced danger every day. Yet it was their way of life, and they made the most of it.

It was also our way of life for fourteen years as we followed the rigs and saw the country. We lived in the Wyoming and Montana mountains and on their prairies, with their summer beauty and winter wonderlands. We also saw their other side—a vicious display of electrical storms that literally made our hair stand on end. We saw jagged streaks of lightning split huge trees down the middle and set a forest ablaze. We knew the raging blizzards that swept out of the north and east, burying the land with drifting snow that could take life without mercy. We learned to respect the elements of weather that affected our lives and the lives of the men who provided for us.

Each state has its own memories: California, Oregon, Louisiana, Wyoming, Montana, and Texas. We lived near drilling sites up and down the California coast. Once near Newhall we visited a western town with a facade built for filming movies. We enjoyed taking the boys to watch movie stars at work. East Whittier, Pismo Beach, and Los Olivias were a few of the places we lived that were interesting and wonderful to explore. We made friends as we became a part of the communities for brief periods.

In New Iberia, Louisiana, the special treat was the savory food. Our favorite pastime was traveling to Cajun country and finding little restaurants where we went into the kitchen and filled our plates with food from the kettles on the stovetop. The ingredients were unfamiliar but always delicious.

We had gone to drilling sites in Oregon when the company pulled its rigs for repairs, putting my husband and others out of work. My husband had family in Yoncalla, so we stayed there. He joined his uncle Jess, a tree topper, working in the woods. This was beautiful country. Jim was five when he decided to begin first grade at Duck Egg School on the Umpqua River— the first of twenty-one schools he would attend before college. Later, the work hours in logging were shortened by the cold and rainy weather, so my husband went back to work for the drilling company and we moved to Montana.

While we were living in Grass Range, Montana, my husband was working seven days a week drilling a well nearby. I decided to buy and operate a café in this friendly little town. We called it Sutter's Café (how original). It was in a hotel with a bar, so we had some built-in customers, but there were also many ranchers nearby. A major highway ran through the town, and the high school was close by, so the café became the hangout for the kids at lunchtime and after school. They were a great bunch of kids, and one spring they gave me a part of my teenage years that I had missed.

When I was in high school, because of my erratic attendance and lack of social life as a result of prejudice against Indians, I never attended a school prom. When the Grass Range students heard that, they invited me to their prom. My family thought it was a great idea. I bought a prom dress and was given a corsage, and two senior boys escorted me to the high school prom. It was a marvelous experience. The band was great, and the gym was beautifully decorated. I danced every dance and enjoyed my delayed prom with a wonderful bunch of kids. Naturally, we ended up at Sutter's Café for hamburgers after the dance, and then we watched the sun come up. It was a perfect way to end a night to remember.

When the wells were finished in the county, I sold the café, and we moved to Roundup, Montana, as they were going to be drilling in Melrose County. We decided it was time to add to our family. This pregnancy was delightful. I had no morning sickness, much to the disgust of friends who had experienced no such luck. Jim was enjoying school, Dennis was a busy toddler, and our family had lots of friends. We were excited about welcoming a new baby.

On a cold, windy afternoon in late November, I knew it was time to pack the suitcase and go to the hospital—which was fifty miles away in Billings, ordinarily about an hour's drive. My husband wasn't due home until four o'clock, but I thought that if we left as soon as he arrived, we would have plenty of time. With each passing pain, though, I became more worried.

Finally, I heard his car and met him at the door. I grabbed him and said, "Get in the car and let's go." He didn't argue. As we left town, it started to snow, and the wind shifted to the north and was blowing with a vengeance that didn't bode well for travel. About twenty miles out, my husband asked if I was okay. I clenched my fists, gritted my teeth, and said "Just drive!" We went ten more miles, and the storm worsened; the wind seemed to come from all directions. All we could see was blowing snow, with an occasional glimpse of the road. My husband said, "Honey, I'm sorry, I can't go any faster. I can't see the road. Are you okay?" Again, between a groan and a moan, I said "Just drive!"

The lights of Billings finally came into view, and we crept up to the hospital still blinded by gusts of snow. The staff met me at the emergency entrance, and my husband left to park the car. When he returned he was met by a nurse who announced, "Congratulations, you have a beautiful new daughter." We named the baby Vicki, and she quickly became dearly loved by our family and friends. The Creator had blessed us with three children. Now our family was complete.

We began to spend less time in the oil fields. As my children grew older, we spent more time in Texas near their grandparents. My husband went to Guatemala to drill wells, and I graduated from nursing school. When he returned from Central America he left the oil fields for good, we thought. He became a policeman in Hereford, Texas. I worked as a private nurse for a doctor in a medical and surgical clinic, and we bought a home in the suburbs and did all the usual things families do in suburbia.

Jim had quit college and married young. He and his wife had returned from Washington, D.C., where he worked for the FBI. We were enjoying our first grandchild, Jaimie Beth, who has never lost her special place in my heart. Dennis left college because he thought he should serve in the Vietnam War. Vicki was enjoying her dual roles as cheerleader and leader of her own pack of teenagers who thought the world revolved around them.

My husband was struggling with a drinking problem, and our marriage was suffering from the strain and uncertainty. Outwardly, we were like many other families, with both parents working and making an effort to keep up with daily life. In church on Sunday I thanked the Creator for our good health and prayed for the safety of my son serving in the Marines, grateful that the rest of us were together as a family.

One fine summer day my father came from the reservation in Wyoming to visit us in Texas. He asked me to return to my people. My whole world began to change in a way none of us had ever imagined. I would begin to understand the early teen years in which I had suffered discrimination because I was an Indian. I would return to my Arapaho people, and the healing would begin.

Chapter Thirteen

Granddaughter, the Arapahos believe their people, except for the children, have a forewarning of death four days before it takes place. We also believe one's spirit remains among the people until the fourth day following death. If all is in order, the spirit then moves on to the next world, with the understanding that it may return whenever it is needed. A spirit mind may follow family members over the years for their protection and safekeeping. The Arapahos believe in the immortality of the soul, or spirit, and have many stories that tell of the spirit world inhabitants.

The day dawned crisp and bright that September morning after my death. At first light the people began to stir, moving quietly and sadly, for they knew of my passing. Campfires were started and food was being prepared before the rosy glow of the sunrise washed over the prairie. The female members of my family had stayed up most of the night making preparations for my burial that day.

Two couriers came into camp after midnight and immediately sensed the mourning that was taking place. They dutifully carried their messages to the Chiefs' Council and then slipped away to rest in preparation for their continuing journey to alert other bands of impending trouble on the plains. Word came early to the people from the council lodge that when my burial had been completed, the band would break camp and move east across Nebraska.

My oldest sister took the lead in preparing me for burial. A new buffalo robe was given to the family. That robe and several other animal robes were soaked in water to soften them. My most beautiful buckskin dress and matching beaded moccasins were chosen to dress me in. First, my body was bathed carefully. The smile on my face, softened by death, gave evidence of happiness as I entered a new world, secure in my faith in the Creator. A Holy Man, one of the medicine men who knew me well, came to paint my face, ensuring my full welcome into the other world and into the presence of friends and relatives who had preceded me.

When the women had finished their preparations, people came to pay their last respects. Some spoke softly to me, leaned down to kiss my brow, and covered my hands with theirs. Others gave the mourning cry and stood by my side wailing. Soon, my sisters came and sat close by my body. An elder took a knife and, after rubbing it with charcoal, sawed through their long hair, cutting it off at shoulder length. Cutting their hair too short would bring bad luck. The cut hair would be put in a bag and buried with me as confirmation of their love. It would be days before they would comb or brush their hair as normal. My two sisters stepped outside the lodge and continued wailing as they took sharp stones and gashed their arms and legs. They had lost a dearly beloved sister and were stricken with grief.

Inside, the Medicine Man spoke to the people and told them of my life and the kind deeds I had done for others. He told how I had fulfilled my duties as a mother and how well I had accepted the duties of a chief's wife and served the tribe. Soft murmurs of assent came from the crowd that had gathered, and he began to pray. My husband stood close by, looking straight ahead with unseeing eyes as he struggled with his grief. His hair, always neatly wrapped in two plaits, now hung loose about his face. This was the way traditional men showed humility before the Creator during their period of mourning.

When the people had left the lodge, my body was wrapped gently from head to foot in the buffalo robe, which was still damp and pliable. Strong thongs of rawhide held the robe securely in place. The other robes were brought forth and wrapped in tight layers around my body. Again, rawhide thongs were wound tight to hold the robes secure.

Since the Arapaho band was traveling, the family chose to have my gravesite located high in the rocky top of a nearby butte. The butte rose up in stark contrast to the rolling, sagebrush-covered hills of the prairie. From the top, one could look in four directions with a wonderful view of the surrounding countryside.

The quiet crowd of friends and relatives followed the men who carried my body up the winding path made by the four-legged of the locality to the burial site. It was not the way of the Arapaho to place their people underground; they laid the body close to Mother Earth. Some of my most precious articles were laid beside me. The belief is not that I would take them with me but rather that my spirit would have use of spirit replicas of the articles in my new life. Rocks were placed to cover the gravesite, followed by a covering of thornbushes and brambles to discourage animals from bothering the area until Mother Earth had claimed me in my entirety.

As the crowd started back to camp, the wailing of the women increased in intensity, and for a time the grief and sorrow in their voices rang out across the prairie to let all creation know of their suffering.

It was still early morning as the people gathered for the Paint Ceremony. They were living in uncertain times, with the constant threat of war, so it was necessary to have the ceremony before they moved camp. Tradition held them there until everything was completed in a good way. The Paint Ceremony was also called a cleansing, intended to enable family members to return to their regular duties and go about as before. The ceremony would allow my husband to choose his period of personal mourning yet still maintain his leadership role in protecting the tribe. The ceremony must be done in the morning to allow for a day of sunshine to watch over everyone.

There were no other sounds across the rolling grassland as the low, steady beat of the drums brought the people to their knees. Each person was wiped off, or cleansed, by one who had earned that honor and proven himself worthy. The Medicine Man and his chosen helpers carefully painted each face in the traditional manner with sacred red paint. Family members and friends would still mourn for me, but now they had permission to continue their life as before.

As the people broke camp anticipating a long day's travel, my sisters prepared food to leave at the burial site. They pounded elk meat into fine particles and mixed it with berries. Adding a little soft buffalo fat, they easily shaped the mixture into patties. They walked to the burial site and dug a small hole in which to bury the food. They talked softly to me, telling me about the food and asking me not to feel bad because they were leaving. Tears were streaming down their faces as they walked away, knowing in their hearts that they might never return to that spot. They had done what they could to show how much they loved me, and now they had to leave.

The constant flow of white people into the Indian homeland and the chaos resulting from the battles caused many Indian people to be torn away from those they loved. They often had to leave family members buried alone on the prairie. This is not the traditional way. Arapahos prefer to visit the graves and look after their loved ones.

There is comfort in being able to sit quietly by the grave and converse with the loved one and decorate the site with flowers or plants. This provides a sense of having spent time with those who are gone. Their spirits understand, and we believe they find their families at times and do not forever roam the hills restlessly.

The site of my grave is high on a butte in Nebraska, probably unknown to the people who now cross the prairie. But my people do not forget me, and when my spirit comes to visit, in the sweat lodge or the Sun Dance camp, I will be welcomed. As the Arapahos move forward with their lives, they still like to gather for storytelling and to honor those who have gone to the other side. *Ho hou.*

Thank you, Grandmother Goes In Lodge, for your contribution to the history of our people.

Chapter Fourteen

Grandmother, our move from Texas to Wyoming in 1969 was understood to be permanent. This was a serious undertaking and involved a lot of changes within the family. My oldest son, Jim, with his wife, Jan, and baby, Jaimie Beth, decided to move north with us, and we were pleased to have them join us. Dennis would soon be discharged from the Marines and would also join us in Wyoming. Vicki was leaving a school where she was involved in many activities and had many friends. All that would change as she became a freshman in a new school.

But our family is resilient, and after we had sold our home and headed north we began to look at the move as an adventure. One of Vicki's friends had come to supper one evening and then settled in to stay for several months. Her parents were on a yacht somewhere in the Gulf of Mexico, and she preferred to live with us rather than be looked after by servants. She was devastated by our decision to move. She ended up moving to Wyoming with us.

We chose Lander as our first location near the reservation. Everyone found jobs, as is the pattern in our family. We had a great summer, making new friends and exploring the countryside. When fall came we reluctantly sent Vicki's friend back to her parents in Texas. We cried when she left and wished we could have kept her in the family.

Vicki enrolled at Lander High School and quickly made friends. She had been a cheerleader for two years in Texas. Now she spent the next four years cheering for a new group of athletes. She also joined the school's Indian Club and began her own cultural awareness program. Dennis was discharged from the Marines and returned home. After a brief period he found a job and prepared to return to school, planning to attend a teachers' college in Nebraska. When the administration there insisted that he cut off his braids, he moved to Denver and eventually graduated from Metropolitan State College. Jim worked at the radio station and enjoyed having his own afternoon show. Later, he became the news anchorman. His family soon welcomed two boys, Jon and Jeff, into their home. I was excited to be the grandmother of three beautiful children.

We saw my dad frequently, and I would ask him, "What is it that you want me to do?" He would reply, "Get acquainted with your people, and you will know what to do when the time comes."

The days went by quickly. Everything was changing. When I first went back to Wyoming I continued my nursing career at the local hospital. Unfortunately, I broke my foot playing basketball, so I took a job managing a discount store where I could prop my foot up on a chair and still work.

One afternoon some people from the reservation came to see me and asked if I would build a grocery store on the reservation. So I built a supermarket in Ethete, an Arapaho community located in the middle of the reservation. The building project was put together through the combined efforts of the Bureau of Indian Affairs (BIA), the Small Business Administration, and tribal programming. It was a terrific learning experience, as well as a successful venture.

My father enjoyed coming into the store with his friends, and they would visit and laugh as they shared stories. The store's meat department was greatly appreciated, particularly by the men who bought fresh kidneys and ate them on the spot. Indian people love tripe (the inside lining of a cow's stomach), and it makes a delicious soup when cooked the Indian way.

I bought the tripe from a meatpacking house. When it arrived it was glistening white and packed in wrapped squares. The men used to tease me and tell me it would sell better if I dragged it through a corral a few times before presenting it to customers. I presumed this was a reflection on old-time ranch meat processing.

I began to notice something amazing. The store would be filled with Indian people shopping, visiting, and laughing. The men told lots of stories with appropriate hand gestures. The store would be a very noisy and exciting place. Then a white person would come into the store, and there would be instant silence. People continued to shop, but no words would be exchanged. When the non-Indian left, the talking and laughter would resume. I could always tell without looking up when a non-Indian came in the door.

In this store my Arapaho cultural learning became more important than the business at hand. My father would send elders in to talk to me, old women and old men, all wise in the ways of what it meant to be an Arapaho. You must do this, you may not do this, and so forth. Best of all, they always explained why or why not rather than just saying something should or should not be done. I learned to listen while they talked because I learned so much.

A medicine man came in with my dad one day. He went to each corner of the store, all the way around, making gestures and talking (praying) to himself. I asked my dad what he was doing, and he told me, "You should be very proud. He is blessing your store." Later the man came in and asked to borrow a few dollars. He needed to make a trip somewhere to do a cedaring or a doctoring and needed travel money. He said he would pay me back when he returned, as they would gift him for his services. True to his word, he came back and repaid the money.

Several years later I was working in the hospital again when they brought this medicine man in with a serious illness. He remembered me and asked that I stay with him during the medical procedures. I was happy to do so. We visited often, and I listened carefully to what he had to say. Very early one morning I dreamed that one of the elders came to me and said the medicine man was dying. I woke instantly and told my husband about the dream. He suggested I go to the hospital. When I got there I was told the man had just passed away. I believe the dream was his way of telling me he was leaving this world.

In 1973, during the time I was operating the store, my husband's drinking habits became too much for me, and we divorced. I continued to operate the supermarket, and it was during this tumultuous time that I learned about the complexity of tribal jurisdiction. A white man, who had been drinking, came into the store and became quarrelsome. He was upsetting the store personnel, and I asked him to leave. He refused. I called the Tribal Police to have them ask him to go home. When they arrived, they refused to order him to leave. They informed me that he was a white man on the reservation, and they had no jurisdiction over him. I would have to call the County Sheriff's Department and have them send someone out. I called them and they said, "We can't go into an Indian-owned store on reservation trust land and do anything."

I was losing patience. I stood up and said, "Get out of my way. I will throw him out myself, and you big boys in uniform can stand there and watch me!" I guess I challenged their pride because they said, "Okay, okay, we'll do it. Please sit down." The whole situation was so ludicrous that the white man's good humor returned, and we all had a good laugh as he left. I never forgot that encounter in later years as I worked through jurisdictional issues for tribal people.

I had worked with some of the members of the Shoshone and Arapaho Joint Tribal Business Council when we were building the store. I watched the administration of tribal affairs with interest. One intriguing member of the Arapaho Business Council caught my attention. When I first met Nellie Scott, I thought she was amazing. She was small in stature but big in personality and full of vim and vigor. She loved challenges, and she loved her people. Because she was not a full-blooded Arapaho, some Arapaho people gave her a bad time about being oriented to whites. She resented this implication, but it never held her back from doing the work she loved—working for the betterment of her people. In fact, I believe the adversity made her stronger because she had great confidence in the ability of the Arapaho to survive and do well. And she would help show them the way.

Nellie Scott was appointed to the first Northern Arapaho Council and remained a member for more than twenty years. She shared many stories with me about those early days. The first council meeting was held in the basement of the BIA building, dimly lit with spiderwebs draping the walls. It began as a Joint Business Council, involving both tribes. The Shoshone and Arapaho tribes then each formed individual business councils.

Nellie detested the alcohol abuse among our people and the disgraceful effects it had on behavior. A bar was built on the reservation, with the excuse that our people were going to drink anyway, and it was better if they drank close to home. They would not be driving home to the reservation in an intoxicated state, perhaps killing themselves or others. A bar called "The Blue Bull" was located near Nellie's house.

She kept five dogs, each fiercely dedicated to its role as her protector. It was amazing to see this tiny woman move determinedly among the dogs who would be jumping, snarling, and snapping at each other in their haste to attack. She would invite me to the house to visit, telling me the dogs would not touch me as long as she was there. Many times I sat tentatively perched on the edge of the chair as five pairs of beady eyes watched me with drooling tongues hanging out and, I believed, ready to pounce at any moment.

Some brave drinkers would go to her house to harass her, to complain, or to beg for more drinking money. One night she had seen enough of these untimely visits. She took the rifle she kept behind the door and shot it through the floor. The noise was horrendous, and even the dogs scattered to the kitchen. Then she yelled, "The next shot goes through the door. If you're on the porch, that's your tough luck!" That put a stop to the night visits.

Nellie was a huge source of information. She knew just about everything that went on throughout the reservation. She knew the political side of Indian affairs and kept in close contact with community members and their needs. She became my mentor, and I listened carefully to all she had to say. One day she said, "You see how it is here on the reservation. We are still learning how to get along with the white man and his ways. What you need

Virginia J. Sutter, author, in traditional Northern Arapaho dress, 1994. Courtesy, Spotted Horse Collection.

to do is divorce that alcoholic husband of yours, go back to school, and come home and serve your people in the best way you can." I laughed and continued operating the store. It is ironic that a short time later I did exactly what she had suggested. She lived to see me divorced and back in school. I imagine she was thinking "I told you so." She died while I was away at school. Ten years later I often longed for her support and advice when I became a member of the Northern Arapaho Business Council.

During my third year of owning the store, I met a Southern Cheyenne/Arapaho man from Oklahoma. He was a policeman for the city of Lander, and after a brief courtship we married and I closed the store. By this time my daughter was about to graduate from college and marry the love of her life, John. We welcomed this handsome young man from Minnesota into the family. Within a few years they had two boys, Matthew and Ben. Dennis met and married Jeanne, a charming Irish lass from Michigan. Their family grew to include a daughter, Keli, and two sons, Michael and Ryan. I now had eight grandchildren to enjoy over the years.

While I was operating the supermarket at Ethete, it became apparent that the Arapaho and Shoshone tribes that shared the reservation had never resolved their original hostility toward one another. This affected the efficiency of the federal government programs designed to provide services to the tribes. Of special interest to me were the alcohol and drug programs, which appeared ineffectual. In fact, people called them the "three hots and a cot" program, which dried out the drunks, filled them full of food and vitamins, and then sent them out—only for them to return to the same drinking habits. I thought many times about my brother and his struggle for life. I had other relatives who were fighting alcoholism and wondered if these programs could be more successful. I regretted my lack of education because I knew the government funding was one piece in solving the problem, but the programs themselves were unsuccessful. What would it take to turn them around?

When I told my children I wanted to go back to school to get the education I needed to develop better programs to meet the needs of our people, they were both surprised and pleased. When each of them started college, I had told them I would be there to help them but that I would like to see them get scholarships and pay their own way through school. And they did. Now they said, "We'll be here for you, Mom, but let's see if you can work your way through school." And I did.

My second husband, Ted, had always promoted education among Indian people. Unfortunately, that belief did not apply to his wife. I was apprehensive about meeting the requirements of higher education. His support would have been appreciated, but he negated my efforts. There were other problems in our marriage. He had been sober for seven years when we met, but the return to police work appeared to facilitate his return to drinking. After four years of an on-again, off-again marriage, I set his shoes outside the apartment door. Being a traditional Indian, he asked, "Does this mean what I think it does?" I replied, "Yes, I am packing to leave and will be returning to school full-time. Our marriage is over."

The next ten years, Grandmother Goes In Lodge, tested my tenacity. How much did I want more education to serve my people? I wanted it enough to withstand long hours of study, the uncertainty of having enough money for books, often working three jobs at a time to earn enough money to stay in school. But I earned several degrees: first an A.S. in science, a B.S. in sociology, an M.S. in social work, and a Ph.D. in public administration in 1995.

Finally, I thought I was ready to serve American Indian people. Nearly all my jobs during college had been with Indian agencies. The one exception was teaching at the university, but even there I usually had Indian students.

Meanwhile, my father had passed away. He was never specific about what he wanted me to do. He would only say, "Just work with and for your people and other Indians. You will learn to understand the needs of the people and know what to do when the time comes." As I look back over the years and think of the American Indian tribes I have worked with and for, I hope I am fulfilling his wishes.

After serving as chief executive officer (CEO) of the American Indian Center in downtown Oklahoma City, I worked with the Cheyenne/Arapaho Tribe as its health administrator. When I was offered a position with my

Virginia J. Sutter, author, receiving doctorate degree, University of Oklahoma, Dr. Larry Hill attending, 1995. Courtesy, Spotted Horse Collection.

own Arapaho Tribe in Wyoming, I decided it was time to return home to the Wind River Reservation.

It was strange to return. I was single, with no family obligations, full of energy, and very well trained academically. I was ready to work, but I was not welcomed with open arms. An educated Indian returning to the reservation is regarded with suspicion and prejudice. One hears unjust, demeaning remarks—you are like the white man, too good for your friends and relatives. Such remarks were directed not just at me. I also saw them leveled against younger students when they returned home. Many received a better reception off the reservation among non-Indians, so they accepted jobs there and left home.

We lost well-educated and well-meaning Indian college graduates to the outside world because they were not accorded a decent welcome when they returned to the reservation. This was happening not just on our reservation. In later years I observed other tribes doing the same thing. Many times I have heard great speeches by tribal officials about educating our children—they are our future leaders, and so on. But when the young people do receive an education, they are not always welcomed with jobs on their own reservations.

I was ignored for about three months, but I enjoyed my job in research and development for the tribe, and gradually people began to speak to me. Friendly interaction increased. After about a year some elders asked if I would run for the Business Council. Tribal affairs lacked business accountability, and the elders thought it was time for a change.

I had taught political science at the university level, so I was familiar with political activities in the white man's world. I was not particularly interested in American Indian politics, especially not bad politics. Changes within the Business Council usually set off a flurry of political activity that went beyond the norm.

Challenge was the key word. Could I make a difference, and could I restore some of the credibility the tribe had lost, both locally and nationally? I accepted the challenge, which led to five years of disorder and political conniving before I became an effective leader in Indian affairs. The elders wanted change from corruption to more traditional behavior. Traditionally, Arapaho people have been considered honest and respectful, never individually oriented but looking after what is best for all tribal members. That is one of the attributes that keeps us a strong and respected nation among other Indian tribes. Arapaho people never steal from one another.

I was elected to the Business Council and had the distinction of being the second woman in Arapaho tribal history to serve as chairperson of the Northern Arapaho Business Council. Nellie Scott was the first.

Our story, Grandmother Goes In Lodge, is about our lives and Arapaho tradition, the differences between your time and mine. Indian politics and mayhem are not about tradition, so that is another story. I will tell you only that it was a difficult time. My life was threatened. People were sent to beat me up. Through it all, I learned that it takes only a small group to undermine an entire tribe's integrity and accountability. But during the five years of my involvement with the Business Council, credibility was restored, budgets were balanced, the dishonesty that had run rampant for several years was blasted from the front page of the newspapers, and there were no secrets from the tribe. Tribal members were promised retribution, and another Business Council, with newly elected members, moved ahead. I returned to working on health issues with the Indian Health Service, and my life returned to some degree of normalcy.

In 1996 I visited the elders who had asked me to become politically involved and requested permission to leave the reservation and spend a year in the Seattle area where my children and grandchildren lived. I wanted to get better acquainted with my grandchildren before they grew up. The elders agreed that I had done what they had asked and wished me well. I spent the first year in Washington working with an Indian tribe in the far northwestern corner of the state and began to learn more about the Coastal cultures, which are so different from our Plains culture.

In Washington state I concentrated mostly on developing health and human services for Indian tribes. Government officials in Washington are much more receptive to working with Indian tribes than those in other states I have been involved with over the years. Following my work with the Coastal tribes, I became the CEO/administrator of a Nevada tribal hospital before returning home to the reservation in 2002. In 2003, continuing my work among the Indian people, I accepted the position of

CEO/administrator for the Pit River Tribe, one of the largest tribes in northern California. I am learning more every day. And I believe I am following my father's wish that I dedicate my life to working for Indian people.

Today, my children are healthy and prospering. I have eight grandchildren and three great-grandchildren. I return to the reservation every year for the Sun Dance ceremonies. A few years ago I gathered all my family— twenty-three in all—into a Sun Dance camp and explained that it would soon be time for them to accept the responsibility of carrying on the tradition of continued support of the Arapaho Sun Dance ceremonies.

Regarding tradition and cultural expectations, tell me, Grandmother Goes In Lodge, as I move forward with my life, am I fulfilling your expectations of how you would want your great-granddaughter to live in today's world with respect to the traditional Arapaho way? I ask your blessing.

Epilogue

Grandmother Goes In Lodge, I find it very sad that you missed being by your husband's side to see his many exciting and honorable achievements during his lifetime. To become a chief among the Arapaho was not hereditary; the individual had to earn the honor. Chief Sharp Nose attained the rank of monarchical chief. He became famous for his leadership, which was marked by thoughtfulness. The U.S. Army cited him as a forceful Indian leader who thought clearly and was true to his word.

You were there for the parting of the tribes in the spring of 1876, when some Arapahos were sent to Oklahoma and Chief Sharp Nose and his Northern Arapahos moved to Fort Robinson. It was on this trip to make the winter camp that you became ill and made your journey to the other world.

You were not destined to be with him when he volunteered his services in General George Crook's detachment of Indian scouts of the Ninth U.S. Army Cavalry in Fort Smith, Nebraska. He did this to protect his people; he understood only too well the pressures created by the continued inflow of white people into Arapaho territory. Camping was very different from the early days, but his two wives stayed close by his side. The buffalo were gone, and hunting for food was difficult. The peaceful prairie was now criss-

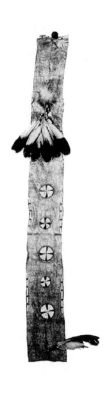

A ceremonial "no retreat sash," Northern Arapaho, and collected in Sharp Nose's camp. N.d., but probably c. 1880. The sash is of buckskin embellished with five quilled discs and eagle feathers. It went over the warrior's head and onto the battlefield; the end was pinned to the ground beyond which custom decreed he must not retreat. Courtesy, National Anthropological Archives, Smithsonian Institution (neg. no. NHB-30031).

crossed by noisy trains, their black smoke pouring forth from their engines. The choices for summer and winter camps were changing, as Indians' land decreased and they were crowded out of their former spaces. The freedom of travel over the Great Plains would never be the same.

You missed seeing your daughter Caroline marry a second time after her first husband died. She moved into Arapaho country in Wyoming, finally settling on the Wind River Reservation where she married again. She had three children with her second husband, an Arapaho with some Gros Ventre ancestry. My father was her third child, and thus I became your great-granddaughter.

The Northern Arapahos settled on the Wind River Reservation in 1878. I don't believe you would have liked moving onto a reservation and losing the freedom of life on the prairie, camping wherever it best suited the tribe— where the hunting was good, the air fresh, and the rivers clean and uncontaminated, the shores free of beer cans and other refuse now left by humans. You lived your life in a wonderful era, a time when it was good to be an Arapaho, respected by the other tribes—even those you called enemies.

I would like to visit with you about the changes that have taken place on our reservation. Alcohol and drug abuse has taken a terrible toll on our people. Respect for elders and the traditional courtesy among extended families have diminished. But there are some wonderful, caring people on the reservation. Many of the older people still hold strictly to the traditional ways.

There are medicine men who still practice their ways to heal and serve the people. The prayers are still offered in a true spiritual manner. I believe the spirits of the Old Ones come to be with us and to hear the sweat songs once again. They hear the prayers sent up to the Creator in the steam from the water poured over hot rocks. They make their presence known to many of us in the sweat lodge. Perhaps the spirit of Grandmother Goes In Lodge also comes. We are glad for their presence, and we make them welcome.

There are many sweat lodges. It is not uncommon to see these low, round structures, made of bent willows and covered with blankets, being built in the backyards of people's homes. Almost every weekend a sweat lodge is held somewhere on the reservation. Some are called "cowboy sweats," intended mainly for prayer and purification, but many are run by ceremonial people who maintain the traditional ways.

The Sun Dance time comes every year. There are only outward changes, those in the campground. The chosen eighty-acre site is filled with tepees and shades, as it was in your time; but now there are also cars, motor homes, and other modern vehicles. But when the drums start and the people gather, the intent and purpose remain the same. The dancers fulfill a vow by fasting and dancing for the three days and nights. This vow is made to the Creator to gain a favor, to ward off serious danger, or as a thanksgiving offering. The dancers make the vow for themselves, for a family member, or for the tribe.

The Sun Dance has been handed down to us as the Arapaho religion. It is still our way of life, and perhaps this is why we continue to increase our number and remain strong—we are still *Hinon'eino.*

Suggested Readings

This list is offered as suggested reading for those who want to learn more about the early written history of Arapaho people and their culture.

Coolidge, Grace. *Teepee Neighbors.* Boston: Four Seas, 1917.

Dorsey, George A. *The Arapaho Sun Dance.* Publication 75, Anthropological Series 4. Chicago: Field Columbian Museum, 1903.

Dorsey, George A., and Alfred L. Kroeber. *Traditions of the Arapaho.* Publication 81, Anthropological Series 5. Chicago: Field Columbian Museum, 1903.

Eggan, Frederick R. "The Cheyenne and Arapaho Kinship System." In Eggan, *Social Anthropology of North American Tribes.* Chicago: University of Chicago Press, 1937.

Elkin, Henry. "The Northern Arapaho of Wyoming." In Ralph Linton, ed., *Acculturation in Seven American Indian Tribes.* New York: D. Appleton-Century, 1940.

Fowler, Loretta. *Arapaho Politics, 1851–1978: Symbols in Crises of Authority.* Lincoln: University of Nebraska Press, 1982.

Gross, F. "Nomadism of the Arapaho Indians of Wyoming." *University of Wyoming Publications in Science* 15, 3 (1950).

Kroeber, Alfred L. "The Arapaho." *American Museum of Natural History Bulletin* 18, Vol. 13, Pts. 1–4. New York: American Museum of Natural History, 1902–1907.

Mooney, James. "Arapaho." In Frederick Webb Hodge, ed., *Handbook of American Indians North of Mexico. Bureau of American Ethnology Bulletin* 30, 2 vols. Washington, D.C.: Bureau of American Ethnology, 1907.

Trenholm, Virginia Cole. *The Arapahoes, Our People.* Norman: University of Oklahoma Press, 1970.